A COMPENDIUM OF

LINES
FOR ALL
OCCASIONS

KNOCK
KNOCK®
LOS ANGELES, CALIFORNIA

Created, published and distributed by Knock Knock
6080 Center Drive
Los Angeles, CA 90045
knockknockstuff.com
Knock Knock is a registered trademark of
Knock Knock LLC

ISBN: 978-168349092-0
UPC: 825703-50182-7

10 9 8 7 6 5 4 3 2

A COMPENDIUM OF

LINES
FOR ALL
OCCASIONS

Insults

Excuses

Rejections

Mind Games

Put-Downs

Cop-Outs

TABLE OF CONTENTS

A Social Conscience · Personal Style · To the Boss · To Underlings · To Coworkers · To Customers · To Service People

Appearance · Hygiene · Age · Youth · Poor Style · Nuts & Crazies · Cheats & Liars · Dunderheads · Pessimists · Optimists · Bores · Losers · Assholes, Egomaniacs & Narcissists · Hipsters · Pseudo-Intellectuals · Addictive Types · Ideologues · Slackers & Layabouts · Jerks · Between Parents & Children · Sibling · Extended Family · Bad Friends · Lovers · Lotharios & Leches · Sluts & Romantic Rivals · Bureaucrats and Public Authorities · Coworkers · Overlings & Underlings · Lousy Parents · Citizens with Poor Manners · Celebrity Catcalls

Workplace Laziness · Blame Technology · Tardiness · Firing Someone · To a Minion · Office Etiquette · Cheating Hearts & Other Parts · Generally Bad Behavior · Eschewing Responsibility · Dumping a Date · Forgot Anniversary · Not Moving In ·.Falling Asleep in an Untimely Manner · Not in the Mood · Breakups · Child to Parent · Parent to Child · Avoiding Chores · Excusing Non-Attendance · Getting Out of Invites · Explaining the Family · General Bad Manners · Roommates · Awkward Moments · Political Correctness · Ingesting Substances · Weight · Food · Career · Love · In Trouble On the Road · In an Inappropriate Place · In School · In the Store · Badly Behaving Pets

INTRODUCTION

—— *Winning the Battle of Wits* ——

The prevailing message in the ether is that we should all try to get along, that we should make an effort to understand points of view very different from our own so we can heal our many divides. Sure. Whatever. But it's not always worth it to smile and play nice. Sometimes the occasion simply demands a snappy insult or put-down, a devious mind game, a glib excuse or cop-out, or a well-timed rejection. If we're to survive our daily interactions with family, coworkers, bosses, and the jerk in line at the DMV, sometimes we're just going to have to go low.

Trouble is, it's hard to come up with the perfect comeback or insult in a given moment. All you can think of are clichés or stock retorts such as, "sez you." *Lines for All Occasions* gives you the bon mots you're looking for. Use these lines when you want to have the last word, cut the tension, or fling an insult that's so witty, your target won't notice how nasty it is. Use one on your kid, spouse, or parent to keep you from completely losing it. Hurl them at the TV or radio when you're hearing a politico spouting nonsense. Toss one into a debate on social media and you'll change someone's mind. (Just kidding, that's impossible.) Memorize your favorites; or consult this book on the sly to find a good put-down.

While the first step is to have the ideal quip at the tip of your tongue, the second is to know how to deliver your barb to the greatest effect (so you hear a mic drop, not a sad trombone).

The BBC provides some guidance, and no one knows how to deliver a witty riposte better than the Brits. They suggest you sharpen your listening skills—really pay attention to what people are saying—so you can perfectly time your response. Take some improv classes if you want to get really good at this. The BBC also notes that the best comeback is one that really speaks the truth. Other ways to deliver a great line? Project confidence, whether you have it or not. Keep it simple. Stay calm: don't show anger or disdain—deadpan is the best way to go. And please, don't laugh at your own joke. You'll just kill the effect.

It's a dangerous world out there. Fortunately, this compendium of *Lines for All Occasions* has all the snark, venom, and wit you remember from the original books, plus a selection of all-new zingers. It will give you the verbal ammunition you'll need to face challenges, come out on top, and leave haters, hecklers, family, friends, and uncouth folks of all kinds laughing to boot.

INSULTS

— *Preparing to Unleash the Beast* —

Whether you're teeming with frustration, overwhelmed with envy, or just plain in the mood, there are unlimited reasons to fire off an insult. From four-letter words to long-winded diatribes, backhanded compliments to in-your-face jeers, sometimes you've got to say what's really on your mind. The personal benefits of releasing such negative energy far outweigh someone else's hurt feelings. You'll feel empowered, in control, and generally better about yourself by taking down those around you. In today's world, niceness is totally overrated.

French philosopher Henri Bergson argued that comedy has a corrective purpose, pulling its target back into cultural conformity. Indeed, everyone benefits from constructive criticism. Your truth-telling may sting, but it also might do recipients a favor, perhaps even inspiring a life change—a haircut, a trip to the library, or some serious counseling. We're surrounded by the ugly and the smelly, the crotchety and the immature, the stupid and the pretentious, and someone's got to take the initiative to tell it like it is.

When selecting your words, think about the lines that best reflect your personality, intention, and desired outcome. Direct or slow-burning? Humorous or heinous? Ending or provoking a battle? Also consider your relationship to the insultee and the severity of the offense. Are you faced with an obnoxious jerk with no regard for others? Or are you combating a friend who desperately needs encouragement to get in the shower? In addition, be sure to plan your delivery.

Despite the age-old saying that "words will never hurt me," we all know that a biting comment can be a devastatingly effective slap in the face. It's not easy being mean, but this chapter will increase your self-assurance and establish your superiority. By attacking those who need to be knocked down a peg, you'll make the world a better place—one moron at a time.

"If you can't pronounce it, don't say it."

UGLY

Oh, my God! You look terrible!
Have you been sick?

———————◆———————

You're dark and handsome.
When it's dark, you're handsome.

———————◆———————

I've had a lot to drink, and
you still don't look good.

———————◆———————

You have such a striking face. Tell me,
how many times were you struck there?

———————◆———————

Ah, I understand—you fell out of the ugly tree
and hit every branch on the way down.

———————◆———————

You've got that faraway look.
The farther away I get, the better you look.

A good plastic surgeon could fix that.

If I throw a stick, will you chase it?

I assume you've fired your dentist.

You have such great hair.

You have such a great personality.

HEAVY

Congratulations! What's your due date?

The only thing you can fit into at the
Gap is the dressing rooms.

I remember you when you only had one chin.

On a scale of 1 to 10, you're a 747.

You may not be good at losing weight, but you seem to be pretty good at finding it.

When you go to a restaurant, you don't get a menu—you get an estimate.

Your favorite food must be seconds.

Lycra really should come with a warning label.

Not everyone can bounce back after pregnancy.

I feel honored to have witnessed
your continual growth.

You have real presence.

As a matter of fact,
you do look fat in those pants.

You have such a pretty face.

HEIGHT

You're so short your hair smells like feet.

When it rains, are you always
the last one to know?

I hope you're well compensated elsewhere.

BACKHANDED COMPLIMENT

Some of the most effective insults come in the form of compliments. The recipient will first be flattered, then insulted—a deft one-two punch. Comments such as "You've lost so much weight!" and

"Your hair looks prettier today!" sound like praise, but the insult ("You were so fat!" and "Your hair usually looks awful!") lurks just below the surface. These Trojan horse insults appear harmless but will have the desired effect nonetheless.

HYGIENE

I have two words for you: personal grooming.

———————◆———————

Nice cologne. Must you marinate in it?

———————◆———————

It wouldn't be so bad if your
personal scent wasn't so personal.

———————◆———————

Actually, the unibrow look was never in.

———————◆———————

Do you smell like this on purpose?

———————◆———————

Are you going for the hippie look?

———————◆———————

I never used to floss—until I met you.

May I offer you a mint?

Do me a favor and go through
the car wash—without your car.

STYLE

The eighties called—they want
their wardrobe back.

Whatever kind of look you
were going for, you missed.

You look cheap—was that the point?

You could be charged with
excessive use of denim.

You look like shit. Is that the style now?

Your ensemble does a terrific job
of maximizing your flaws.

I'm sure that would look good on someone.

Is the stripper look in again?

Very classy—visible thong and plumber's crack.

AGING BODIES

The sell-by date on your eggs is about to expire.

For some people, forty is the new twenty-nine,
but I don't think you can pull that off.

Does it take you twice as long
to look half as good?

It's time to start acting your age—old.

You know so much. Too bad you
don't remember anything.

Congratulations on reaching
your second childhood.

The good news is you look like you should be
respected; the bad news is you're not.

You look like a million bucks— all
green and wrinkled.

Why doesn't your face move?

It may be too late for Botox.

What's left of your hair is getting so gray!

———◆———

The only thing you should exercise is caution.

———◆———

It takes you longer to rest than it did to get tired.

———◆———

Don't worry about your weight—when you're
old you look better fat than skinny.

AGING SOCIAL LIVES

It's time you stop looking for Mr. Right and start
looking for Mr. Right Now.

———◆———

If this is your midlife crisis, I guess you're
planning to live to 120.

———◆———

Now that you're old enough to watch your step,
you're too old to go anywhere.

Your idea of happy hour is a nap.

Your little black book only contains
names ending in MD.

You've graduated from totally
hip to total hip replacement.

I'd ask you to go upstairs and make
love to me, but I don't think you're
young enough to do either.

To someone your age, "getting lucky" means
finding your car in the parking lot.

ANCIENT HISTORY

Your social security number must be
in the single digits.

SILENT BUT DEADLY

Anthropologists estimate that over ninety percent of communication is nonverbal. Whatever the situation, the lines in this book can, therefore, take you only so far. For example, if you want to ding someone lightly, smile when you deliver your insult. If the infraction is dire, roll your eyes and snort in disgust. Stand-alone signs such as the middle finger, up yours (fist to upward-bending inner elbow), or chin flick will always help you get the last nonword in.

They've asked you to be on
Antiques Roadshow—to be appraised.

I was at the ancient history museum today
and thought of you.

When you were in school,
history was called "current events."

When you were born, the Dead Sea was just sick.

You're so old, the candles
cost more than the cake.

You're so old, you should buy
calendars one month at a time.

If I told you to act your age, you'd die.

CALLOW YOUTH

You remind me of when
I was young and clueless.

You still think the world owes you.

You still think you can change the world.

You'd need twice as much sense to be a half-wit.

You still think your dreams will come true.

You still think you can have it all.

You still think you know everything.

Your lack of experience is matched
only by your surplus of ego.

You should have grown out of that by now.

Grow up!

JUST PLAIN STUPID

I don't know what makes you so dumb,
but it really works.

If brains were taxed, you'd get a rebate.

Don't get lost in thought—it's
unfamiliar territory.

Don't let your mind wander—it's too
little to be let out alone.

You're so dumb, blondes tell jokes about you.

You're so dumb, your dog teaches you tricks.

You're so dumb, you sold your car for gas money.

It's amazing you can walk upright!

You're so dumb, you think a lawsuit
is something you wear to court.

Brains aren't everything. In fact,
in your case they're nothing.

Ever wonder what life would have been like if
you'd had enough oxygen at birth?

If you were any smarter,
I could teach you to fetch.

You're like one of those idiot savants, except
without the "savant" part.

Ignorance can be cured. Stupid is forever.

GASLIGHTING

When dealing with someone who's a little loony, don't just call him crazy—make him crazy, then follow up by insulting his sanity. The classic 1944 thriller *Gaslight* depicts a woman tricked into thinking she's going mad. Her husband moves objects and dims the gaslights and then denies that anything is happening—hence the term "gaslight," to manipulate a person's perceptions so she will believe she's losing her mind.

If what you don't know won't hurt you, you're practically invulnerable.

Most people live and learn. You just live.

NOT BOOK SMART

I wish I were as smart as you think you are.

If you can't pronounce it, don't say it.

———————◆———————

I'm sorry—I didn't mean to use
so many syllables.

———————◆———————

You really earned that BS degree, didn't you?

———————◆———————

Don't let the facts get in
the way of your opinions.

———————◆———————

You should get a refund
on that college education.

———————◆———————

I'm sure your instincts
make up for your ignorance.

———————◆———————

I'd like to insult you, but you wouldn't get it.

LACKING IN SKILLS

Your mediocrity is unparalleled.

———◆———

Oh, I'm sorry—I didn't realize
I was supposed to laugh.

———◆———

It's not the technology—it's you.

———◆———

The fact that no one understands you
doesn't mean you're an artist.

———◆———

You're the only one who believes in your talent.

———◆———

When the computer said "Press any key
to continue," did you realize there is no
"any" key?

You dance like a straight guy.

One of the defining characteristics of writers
is that they are actually supposed to write.

Talking about it and doing it are two
very different things. At least you excel
at talking about it.

Don't quit your day job.

THE CLASSICS

You're one banana short of a fruit salad.

You're one sentence short of a paragraph.

You're two sheep short of a sweater.

If you spoke your mind,
you'd be speechless.

You're a couple of knights short of a Crusade.

You're a few beers short of a six-pack.

You're a few birds shy of a flock.

You're a few clowns short of a circus.

You're a few eggs short of a dozen.

You're a few feet short of the runway.

You're a few peas short of a pod.

You're a few rungs short of a ladder.

You're a few fries short of a Happy Meal.

You're a few sandwiches short of a picnic.

JERKS AND BITCHES

If I wanted to hear from an asshole, I'd fart.

Do you have to work that hard to be a jerk,
or does it just come naturally?

You used to be arrogant and obnoxious.
Now you're the opposite—obnoxious
and arrogant.

You're not yourself today!
I noticed the improvement immediately.

Martha Stewart thinks you're a bad thing.

I don't think you're an asshole,
but I seem to be in the minority.

If I wanted a bitch as a friend,
I would've gotten a dog.

Your personality is such an effective
birth control device, you must save a
lot of money.

You're not even beneath my contempt.

You're the reason God
created the middle finger.

When you take Viagra, do you get taller?

When people say you're the perfect jerk,
I tell them you're not perfect, but you're
doing all right.

SPECIFIC NEOLOGISMS

Certain put-downs are originated by particular groups to describe unique situations. Some favorites: seagull manager (a bureaucrat who flies in, makes a lot of noise, craps all over everything, and leaves), Velcroid (someone who ghosts a celebrity in order to get into photos), 404 (clueless, from the HTML error message "404 error: File not found"), and whorganic (of or pertaining to the naturally whorish). The possibilities are endless!

EGOS AND ATTITUDES

When someone first meets you, they don't like you. But when they get to know you better, they really hate you.

I bet that attitude of yours was really cool back in high school.

There's Mr. Right, there's Mr. Wrong, and then there's you—Mr. Never Wrong.

I know you're self-made. It's big of you to take the blame!

You're such a smart-ass, I bet you could sit on a carton of ice cream and tell what flavor it is.

Is it hard to find hats for such a big head?

I'm so jealous that you finally found your true love. Unfortunately, they haven't legalized self-marriage yet.

It's hard to get over yourself, isn't it?

NUTJOBS AND FREAKS

I'm guessing you haven't been diagnosed yet.

Your personality's split so many ways you go alone for group therapy.

Have you thought about upping the dosage?

Your mind isn't just twisted—it's sprained.

So, your doctor only diagnosed *one* mental illness?

Your baggage is so heavy
you can't even lug it onto the couch.

You put the psycho in psychology.

ℒIARS AND ℭHEATS

You'd make a great politician.

You're as good as your word,
and your vocabulary sucks.

Calling you a dirty liar would be
an insult to dirty liars.

You're so dishonest, I can't even be sure
that what you tell me are lies.

You're so full of shit, your eyes are brown.

I didn't get why they called it
the rat race until I met you.

———◆———

The only difference between you and a
mosquito is that one is a bloodsucking
parasite and the other is an insect.

———◆———

Your motto is if two wrongs
don't make a right, try a third.

———◆———

You lie like a rug.

———◆———

I can tell when you're lying. Your lips move.

———◆———

You invented fake news.

———◆———

You must get lots of exercise talking
out of both sides of your mouth.

LOSERS AND BORES

Your inferiority complex is fully justified.

Do you want me to accept you as you are,
or do you want me to like you?

I'm trying to imagine
you with a personality.

AVOIDING THE STAIRCASE

The French expression *l'esprit de l'escalier* means "the wit of the staircase": the devastatingly witty comeback concocted after the confrontation, too late to deliver, on the way down the staircase. Germans have coined a similar term: *treppenwitz* (*treppen* means "stairs," *witz* means "wit"). With practice and the lines in this chapter, your goal is to preempt the staircase, issuing your scathing ripostes on point and on time.

Anyone who told you to be yourself
couldn't have given you worse advice.

You remind me of one of those people
in school that no one remembers.

You're one bad relationship away
from having thirty cats.

You're acing "mediocre."

You're so boring,
you can't even entertain a doubt.

You're better than Ambien, and cheaper.

There must be something interesting about you.

FAMOUS LIP

"Prince looks like a dwarf who's been dipped in a bucket of pubic hair." —Boy George

---

"Mick Jagger is about as sexy as a pissing toad."
—Truman Capote

"Is he just doing a bad Elvis pout, or was he born that way?" —Freddie Mercury, on Billy Idol

---

"She's so hairy—when she lifted up her arm I thought it was Tina Turner in her armpit."
—Joan Rivers, on Madonna

"His mouth is a no-go area.
It's like kissing the Berlin Wall."
—Helena Bonham Carter, on Woody Allen

"I never forget a face, but in your case,
I'll make an exception."
—Groucho Marx, target unknown

"He can compress the most words into the
smallest idea of any man I know."
—Abraham Lincoln, target unknown

"If he were any dumber, he'd be a tree."
—Barry Goldwater, on William Scott

"A genius with the IQ of a moron."
—Gore Vidal, on Andy Warhol

"Logically unsound, confused,
and unprincipled, unwise to the extreme."
—Jiang Zemin, on George W. Bush

"He's a nice guy, but he played
too much football with his helmet off."
—Lyndon B. Johnson, on Gerald Ford

"It's a new low for actresses when you have to
wonder what's between her ears instead of her
legs." —Katharine Hepburn, on Sharon Stone

"She's a vacuum with nipples."
—Otto Preminger, on Marilyn Monroe

"He's the type of man who
will end up dying in his own arms."
—Mamie Van Doren, on Warren Beatty

"Paul Newman has the attention span
of a bolt of lightning." —Robert Redford

If I agreed with you, we'd both be wrong.

"I knew her before she was a virgin."
—Oscar Levant, on Doris Day

◆

"For years I've regarded [his] very existence as
a monument to all the rancid genes and broken
chromosomes that corrupt the possibilities of
the American Dream; he was a foul caricature of
himself, a man with no soul, no inner convictions,
with the integrity of a hyena and the style of a
poison toad." —Hunter S. Thompson,
on Richard Nixon

◆

"He can't help it—he was born
with a silver foot in his mouth."
—Ann Richards, on George H. W. Bush

"What other problems do you have besides being unemployed, a moron, and a dork?"
—John McEnroe, to a tennis spectator

———————◆———————

"He bores me. He ought to have stuck to his flying machines."
—Auguste Renoir, on Leonardo da Vinci

———————◆———————

"I have tried lately to read Shakespeare, and found it so intolerably dull that it nauseated me."
—Charles Darwin

———————◆———————

"That's not writing, that's typing."
—Truman Capote, on Jack Kerouac

———————◆———————

"She ran the whole gamut of emotions from A to B." —Dorothy Parker, on Katharine Hepburn

YO' MAMA

Also known as the dozens, capping, and dissing, "yo' mama" has evolved into a call-and-response competitive art form. Insult matches date at least to the eighth century, when Arab poets traded barbs in the town square, collected as *Al-Naqa'id*. And in the Middle Ages, Scots verbally abused one another in flyting contests. Today, "mama" insults target obesity, appearance, and stupidity. As a comeback, simply replying "Yo' mama" is a classic.

"He couldn't ad-lib a fart after a baked-bean dinner." —Johnny Carson, on Chevy Chase

"He is to acting what Liberace was to pumping iron." —Rex Reed, on Sylvester Stallone

"I have more talent in my smallest fart
than you have in your entire body."
—Walter Matthau, to Barbra Streisand

"Her voice sounded like an eagle being goosed."
—Ralph Novak, on Yoko Ono

"Michael Jackson's album was only called *Bad*
because there wasn't enough room on the sleeve
for *Pathetic*. —Prince

Nancy Astor: "Winston, if you were
my husband, I'd put poison in your coffee."
Winston Churchill: "Nancy, if you were my wife,
I'd drink it."

Young man: "I can't bear fools."
Dorothy Parker: "Apparently,
your mother could."

"He was humane but not human."
—e. e. cummings, on Ezra Pound

"Always willing to lend a helping hand
to the one above him." —F. Scott Fitzgerald,
on Ernest Hemingway

"An essentially private man who wished his total
indifference to public notice to be universally
recognized." —Tom Stoppard, on James Joyce

CLASSIC COMEBACKS

Bite me!

Bring it on!

Feel special now?

Take a chill pill.

―――――◆―――――

Talk to the hand.

―――――◆―――――

Up your nose with a rubber hose.

―――――◆―――――

It takes one to know one!

―――――◆―――――

Whatever.

―――――◆―――――

As if!

―――――◆―――――

Am not!

―――――◆―――――

I know you are, but what am I?

I'm rubber, you're glue; whatever you say
bounces off me and sticks to you.

Sticks and stones may break my bones,
but words will never hurt me.

Liar, liar, pants on fire!

Shut your pie hole!

Fail!

Piss off.

Up yours!

THE
INTERNATIONAL HATER

When responding to an insult from an idiot, try using another language to make your opponent feel even more stupid than he or she may actually be. Try "idiot" in Finnish (*tampio*), Portuguese (*abestado*), Hawaiian (*hupo*), Tagalog (*tanga*), or French (*connard*). Consult translation dictionaries for more variations on the theme, or use sign language: make a fist and strike your forehead as though knocking sense into it.

Here's a quarter—call someone who cares.

Thank you for sharing.

Get a life!

Yo' mama.

DEALING WITH MEAN

A sharp tongue is no indication of a keen mind.

———◆———

Did your mother teach you
to treat people like that?

———◆———

Let's switch places: you be funny,
and I'll be an asshole.

———◆———

I will always cherish the initial
misconceptions I had about you.

———◆———

I'm only interested in the
opinions of people I respect.

———◆———

I may be ignorant, but you're stupid,
and I can always study.

You've leapt past your
sell-by date straight into rotten.

People treat others the way they feel about
themselves—it must be hard to be you.

Someday you'll find out the truth:
karma's a bitch.

Wow, you're as mean as everybody says you are.

RESPONDING TO IDIOTS

Did you eat lots of paste as a kid?

Do you do children's parties?

I can see your point,
but I still think you're an idiot.

The next time I need an unsolicited and
uninformed opinion, I'll know where to go.

———————◆———————

That insult is older than your underwear.

———————◆———————

That insult is staler than your breath.

———————◆———————

It must be nice to be free of
the burden of intelligence.

———————◆———————

You have nothing to say,
but you say it so loudly.

———————◆———————

Your lips are moving,
but nothing's coming out.

———————◆———————

I'm blonde. What's your excuse?

CALLING CRAZY OUT

Are you in therapy for that?

———————◆———————

You might want to cut back on the sugar.

———————◆———————

I don't know what your problem is,
but I'll bet it's hard to pronounce.

———————◆———————

My mother told me not to
speak to strange people.

———————◆———————

I see you've set aside this special time to
humiliate yourself in public.

———————◆———————

Cancel my subscription—I can't
deal with your issues.

Any resemblance between your
reality and mine is strictly coincidental.

———————◆———————

Did you not get enough attention at home?

———————◆———————

Are you for real?

STFU

How about a little less talk and
a little more shut-the-hell-up?

———————◆———————

I don't like you—and I always will.

———————◆———————

I'm busy now.
Can I ignore you some other time?

———————◆———————

Don't bother me; I'm living happily ever after.

I don't mind your talking as long as
you don't mind my not listening.

I'd like to give you a going-away present,
but you have to do your part.

I'd like to help you out.
Which way did you come in?

You've obviously mistaken me
for someone who gives a damn.

Is that the best you've got?

That's not what your mama said last night.

Why are you even talking?

Someday you'll go far—and I really hope
you stay there.

There's no need to repeat yourself. I ignored
you just fine the first time.

Yes. I've heard that story before. An hour ago.

THE INSULT BARD

Among other things, William Shakespeare has
gone down in history as creator of the most
original insults ever written. Try an easy-to-
follow method to craft your own: first, choose a
degrading adjective; next, a hyphenated, verb-
derived adjective; and finally, link them with a
rich noun (for example, *dumpy* plus *addle-brained*
plus *sow*). Or, use a direct quote from the master
(say, "poisonous bunch-back'd toad").

Can I borrow your face for a few days?
My ass is going on holiday.

I'd love to rip apart the shallow logic you call a
point, but it's beneath me. As are you.

You should come with a warning label.

If you ran like your mouth, you'd be
in good shape.

Don't go away mad, just go away.

Hey, if you stay very quiet and listen
very closely, you can hear the beautiful
sound of you shutting up.

How about a nice hot cup of STFU?

Remember when I asked for your opinion?
Me neither.

———————◆———————

I've never met someone with such a small mind
inside such a big head.

———————◆———————

As an outsider, what do you think of
the human race?

———————◆———————

Even if you make yourself believe it,
it's still a lie.

———————◆———————

You bore me, and I enjoy watching paint dry.

———————◆———————

Save your breath—you'll need it to
blow up your date.

EXCUSES

— *Preparing to Deliver Effective Deception* —

Excuses and lies are a necessary part of life. Six-month-olds begin their careers as proud fibbers with fake laughter and cries, and it's all downhill from there. In fact, if anyone says they don't lie, they're lying. Scientists have demonstrated that excuses and lies paved our evolutionary path by allowing us simultaneously to advance our own interests and to cement our role within our group. Would we ever get our dream job if we said we couldn't type? Could we maintain our clique status if we said "I hate your new haircut"? Successful lying promotes survival of the fittest—the fittest, of course, are the liars.

Forget about guilt—we're born liars and we die liars. What matters is how we lie in between. The overwhelming daily demands of our personal and professional lives are simply too much to handle without excuses and lies. When it comes to saving friendships, dignity, or our own skins, honesty is, quite simply, overrated. Being truthful can ruin marriages, sabotage negotiations, and possibly bring an end to the world as we know it. In his essay "On the Decay of the Art of Lying," no lesser light than Mark Twain acknowledged, "Everybody lies—every day; every hour; awake; asleep; in his dreams; in his joy; in his mourning." The question is not whether to lie or tell the truth—the question is how to lie well.

In this chapter, you'll find help for the workplace, friendships and dating, family and other loved ones, your own inner thoughts, and infractions such as unpaid bills. Finally, because famous people lie more than the average prevaricator, we present you with an inspiring panoply of excuses and lies from the best of the best.

From the most stuttering rationalizer to the baldest-faced fabricator, this chapter will not only provide the best falsehoods for the widest variety of situations, it will help those who still value honesty to shed that useless mantle and get with the human program. Whether or not you believe all this, of course, is up to you—for all you know, we could be lying.

"I have it in my calendar for next week."

WORKPLACE TARDINESS

I'm okay now, but I actually
threw up on the way over here.

———◆———

The toilet overflowed and
I had to wait for the plumber.

———◆———

I had another panic attack.

———◆———

For some reason, my alarm
didn't go off this morning!

———◆———

Traffic was a nightmare.

———◆———

I was dealing with a personal matter.

———◆———

It takes hours to look this good!

PLAYING HOOKY

The cable's out, and I have to wait
all day for the technician to arrive.

It's most contagious in the early stages, and I
don't want to expose everyone at the office.

My husband's eighty-four-year-old
great-aunt died suddenly.

I can't find my car.

I feel a migraine coming on.

I'm dedicating the rest of the day to self-care.

Two words: bad clams.

I couldn't find my keys anywhere.

The vet said I had to watch Mr. Piddles all day to make sure he doesn't have a bad reaction to the medication and die.

———◆———

My briefcase was filled with work I took home, and when I bent down to pick it up, I threw my back out.

MISSED DEADLINE

Didn't we cancel that project?

———◆———

I need an assistant to help me keep track of things like this.

Nothing short of perfect will do for you.

I left it at my friend's house and
she's out of town for a month.

I have it in my calendar for next week.

Everybody else failed to
get me what I needed in time.

I tried so hard, but no matter what I did,
I couldn't finish the project and take my
government-mandated ten-minute breaks.

You didn't authorize overtime.

Every time I thought about the project,
it stressed me out.

ADDED EMPHASIS

When it's necessary to add credibility to your lie, it's easy to amplify your statement with one of these phrases:

- "You have my word on it."
- "I swear on my mother's grave."
- "I swear on the life of my first-born child."
- "I'm looking you in the eye."
- "Now, I'm going to tell you the truth."
- "If you don't believe me, you can have your money back."
- "Look at this face—would I lie to you?"
- "Pinky swear."

I delegated that!

The schedule was completely unrealistic.

It's a moving target, and I want the information
to be as up-to-the-minute as possible.

Do you want it quick, or do you want it right?

I did my best. That's all you can ask.

I have it right here.
Wait—where did that file go?

I'm waiting for the muse to strike.

I've determined that this work
just isn't necessary.

I was one-hundred percent sure I'd already
finished that.

20ᵗʰ-CENTURY SCAPEGOAT: TECHNOLOGY

I accidentally deleted it.

I ran out of paper.

Someone hacked into the file server over SSH
using a crypt-hash attack and placed a root kit
that caused a buffer overrun precipitating a
failure of AFP. As a result, the server unmounted,
and unfortunately I hadn't saved my document.

Didn't you get it? I emailed the whole thing
to you from my home computer last night.

Really? It works on my machine.

I totally, like, fried my motherboard.

The file was mysteriously corrupted.

I have bad news—the system error was fatal.

I'll have my IT guy look into
it and get back to you.

Because of my outsize social media presence,
I was hacked by the Russians.

SLEEPING ON THE JOB

My keyboard was making
the strangest noise.

So funny that you would walk in at this very
moment! I was just meditating on the strategic
initiatives with respect to our core competencies.

Could you turn the heat down a tad?

———————◆———————

I find that a fifteen-minute power nap improves
my overall time management immeasurably.

———————◆———————

Some idiot made decaf.

———————◆———————

It's okay. I'm still clocking these as billable hours.

———————◆———————

One second I was smelling my pen,
and the next second you were waking me up!

———————◆———————

My chiropractor told me to rest my neck
periodically in order to avoid having to
make a worker's comp claim.

———————◆———————

Too many carbs at lunch.

Lucid dreaming is part of
my brainstorming technique.

———————◆———————

I was at the blood bank this morning.

———————◆———————

By accident I took the nighttime medicine.

———————◆———————

It's my break, and I can do what I want with it!

———————◆———————

Amen.

FRIENDSHIP: WHITE LIES

You made that all by yourself?

———————◆———————

I love it!

———————◆———————

Your taste is so eclectic!

The decor really reflects your personality.

It looks so professional!

There's only one word for this—interesting.

No one would ever notice.

I think it's the best thing you've ever written.

Remember—looks aren't everything.

They look totally real!

It's probably just water weight.

DON'T WORK, JUST LIE

Studies show that one-quarter to one-third of all workers tell lies to explain their tardiness or absence. When dallying away from the office, solid excuses and lies are critical, as the same data showed that most managers would be likely to fire employees who were repeatedly late or absent without explanation. Fortunately, nearly three-quarters of employers polled indicated they generally believe the excuses their employees give.

That is so funny.

That is so smart.

You don't look a day over twenty-nine.

Everyone's a little crazy.

FRIENDSHIP: GRAY LIES

Thanks for being so honest.

I didn't know it was a secret!

I won't tell if you won't.

I really like your husband.

I really like your wife.

———◆———

You'll make a great parent.

———◆———

I can always count on you.

———◆———

It was just a misunderstanding.

———◆———

I didn't mean it.

———◆———

BFF!

———◆———

I'd tell you if I thought so.

———◆———

Nothing's wrong.

I'm sure he's just really busy.

Of course I'm not jealous!

I did it for your own good.

OUT OF TOUCH

I've been so crazy at work and just
haven't had a single moment to call you.

As soon as I hit my deadlines, we'll have dinner.

It's so great to hear your voice!
However, I'm in the middle of something.

We're in the honeymoon stage;
it won't always be this way.

I never got your message.

New phone. Who dis?

It's a very busy time of year for me.

It's so hard to find a babysitter.

Has it really been that long?
It doesn't feel like it.

There's just so much TV to watch,
I don't seem to get out much.

Let's meet up after the holidays.

TRUE FASCISM

Alexander Kuzmin, mayor of the Siberian town of Megion, has banned city workers from using certain excuses, including "It's not my job," "I don't know," "It's impossible," and "I'm having lunch." A framed list of all twenty-seven prohibited excuses hangs next to Kuzmin's office. Those who refuse to uphold the ban "will near the moment of their departure." Fortunately, in America, excuse-making is an inalienable right—especially for bureaucrats.

TURNING DOWN INVITATIONS

I'd love to, but I have to work.

I'm completely and utterly exhausted.

I have to wake up early the next day.

That's my weekly night for alone time.

My significant other is having a
total meltdown and needs my help.

I don't have anything to wear.

I think I'm getting sick...soon.

With everything going on in this country and
with this current political climate, you expect
me to celebrate?

UNVITATIONS

It's just an intimate gathering.

It's only family.

It's only immediate family.

I'm not inviting anyone from work.

It's in honor of someone you don't know.

I don't have enough chairs.

It's more of a religious ritual than a party.

It's more of a meeting than a party.

Your invitation must have
gotten lost in the mail.

Party? What party?

ROOMMATES

I cleaned the toilet last time.

———◆———

Those aren't my dirty dishes.

———◆———

I have no idea how your shoes got ruined.

———◆———

I didn't think you would mind.

———◆———

I'll pay you back next week.

———◆———

That beer was yours?

———◆———

I'm just having a few people over.

I have no idea who threw up in the closet.

I thought you weren't coming
home until tomorrow.

He hasn't "moved in with us."
He just sleeps over every night.

We weren't having sex in the
shower—we were trying to conserve water.

I only flush every other time—I'm trying to
conserve water.

GETTING OUT OF DATES

I'm gay.

I'm straight.

I'm married.

I don't date.

You're not my type.

My therapist says you're not my type.

I'm just not ready yet.

You're too good for me.

I didn't mean to slap you. I just saw
your face and had an urge to swipe left.

I have to wash my hair.

DATE SEX

Okay, just a quick drink.

———◆———

The divorce is in the works.

———◆———

I've never done anything like this before.

———◆———

We don't have to do anything
more than cuddling.

———◆———

Of course I'll respect you in the morning.

———◆———

It's only a cold sore.

———◆———

I really think this could go somewhere.

EVERYBODY'S DOING IT

University of Massachusetts psychologist Robert Feldman studied undergraduates to determine everyday lying frequency. He discovered that sixty percent of the subjects lied during a ten-minute conversation; indeed, they told an average of two to three lies per encounter. He also learned that motivations for lying split along gender lines: women tended to lie to make others feel good, while men lied to make themselves look better.

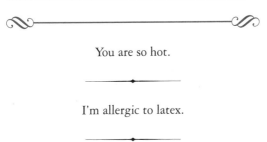

You are so hot.

I'm allergic to latex.

This has never happened to me before.

I'll call you.

He went to doggy heaven.

PARENT TO CHILDREN

This hurts me more than it hurts you.

———◆———

You can do anything you
want if you really try.

———◆———

Daddy was just giving
mommy a special backrub.

———◆———

There are no onions in the lasagna.

———◆———

It tastes just like chicken.

Santa Claus is coming!

———————◆———————

The Tooth Fairy just knows.

———————◆———————

Yes, he's your real father.

———————◆———————

It's what's on the inside that counts.

———————◆———————

If you don't go to college,
you'll end up pumping gas for a living.

———————◆———————

Smoking marijuana is the gateway to meth
addiction. I saw it on the news.

———————◆———————

No one with a liberal arts degree
can get a job in the current marketplace.

The best things in life are free.

———————◆———————

We're almost there.

———————◆———————

You can talk to me about anything.

———————◆———————

It's perfectly normal.

———————◆———————

Of course I trust you.

CHILDREN TO PARENT

I didn't do it.

———————◆———————

Someone made me do it.

———————◆———————

My friend's mom lets him do it.

Everybody's doing it.

No one else's parents ever do that.

Dad said I could do it.

Mom said I could do it.

You didn't tell me not to do it.

I only did it once.

I learned it from you.

She started it.

It was already broken.

I didn't hear you.

I don't feel well.

TIP: BODY LANGUAGE

When delivering a lie—especially to the loved ones who know you best—avoid non-verbal "tells." Lying cues include forced smiles (real smiles involve the muscles around the eyes), formal phrasing (eschewing contractions such as "don't" and "can't"), pitch changes (non-lying vocal levels are relatively even), and erratic eye contact (truth tellers maintain contact, occasionally looking up and to the left, while liars look down and to the right).

We're studying.

We're not doing anything.

Of course grownups will be there.

I don't know.

Nothing.

Nowhere.

You can trust me.

It's not mine.

COUPLES: EVERYDAY

This isn't new—I've had it forever.

———◆———

Your mother is welcome anytime.

———◆———

That dinner was delicious.

———◆———

No, that doesn't make you look fat.

———◆———

I like you with a few curves.

———◆———

No, that really doesn't make you look fat.

———◆———

I don't mind if you go out with your friends.

———◆———

I like your friends.

I'll be ready in a minute.

———◆———

I'll do it in a minute.

———◆———

I thought you were going to do it.

———◆———

I've never heard that story before!

———◆———

Everybody thought it was hilarious.

———◆———

I really want to know.

———◆———

Of course I'm listening.

———◆———

Nothing's wrong.

COUPLES: SEX

I had a hard day at work.

———◆———

I'm tired.

———◆———

I'm sleeping.

———◆———

I have a headache.

———◆———

Maybe later.

———◆———

I ate too much for dinner.

———◆———

Try me again in the morning.

———◆———

It'll only take a minute.

Nobody can hear us.

I just want to express my love for you.

I'll be there in a minute.

I bought you flowers.

I was in the mood—yesterday.

COUPLES: CHEATING

I have to work late.

The Internet provides a
different kind of outlet for me.

We're just friends.

I'll get in bed in a second—
I just need to shower first.

Can you believe my boss scheduled
another business trip?

Oh, we were just joking around in those emails.

I'm not the least bit attracted to him.

I'm not the least bit attracted to her.

The lipstick on my collar? My mother's!

No, that's not women's perfume—
I decided to switch colognes.

It just happened.

I was seduced!

I was going to buy a Porsche for my
midlife crisis, but money was too tight.

BORN LIARS

Humans begin lying shortly after birth. Six-
month-old babies get into the game through fake
crying and laughing. Two months later, they've
added concealment and distraction. At two years
old, toddlers bluff, and by their fourth birthdays
they've discovered the advantages of flattery.
Before they're ten, children will have learned to
cover up a lie—well in advance of their teenage
years, when all that prevarication will truly come
in handy.

Oh, that? It was just someone from work
asking about a deadline. At midnight.

———————◆———————

I'm a child of divorce.

———————◆———————

It didn't mean anything.

———————◆———————

I'll never do it again.

EXCUSES YOU TELL YOURSELF: HEALTH

With the kids, the job, the house,
and the spouse, who has time to exercise?

———————◆———————

If I could afford a personal trainer
and private chef like Gwyneth,
I'd be in great shape, too.

I'm all out of sunscreen.

It's fat-free!

It's carb-free!

It's gluten free!

It's paleo!

It's my cheat day!

It's too hot.

I'll start tomorrow.

EXCUSES YOU TELL YOURSELF: VICES

I'll quit smoking when I have kids.

———◆———

I never buy a pack.

———◆———

If I quit smoking, I'll get fat.

———◆———

I only smoke when I drink.

———◆———

Red wine prevents heart attacks,
but you have to drink a lot of it.

———◆———

Okay, just one drink.

———◆———

The label warned against
pregnant drinking, not *binge* drinking.

I'm just a social drinker.

———————◆———————

I don't drink before noon.

———————◆———————

It's noon somewhere.

———————◆———————

I need to drink—my job is really stressful.

———————◆———————

I need to smoke—my job is really stressful.

———————◆———————

I'm not addicted.

———————◆———————

Cocaine is *organic*.

———————◆———————

It's not speed, it's Adderall.

ANIMAL INSTINCT

Your pets may not always be telling you the truth—lying pervades the animal kingdom. Some frogs lower their croaks to imitate larger frogs, thus attracting more females. Mother birds have been known to feign broken wings to divert predatory attention away from the nest. In one of the most overt displays of cross-species lying, Koko, a sign-language-speaking gorilla, tore the sink off the wall of her pen and then, referring to her pet kitten, signed "Cat did it."

It's not illegal.It shouldn't be illegal.

I'll stop tomorrow.

YOLO!

EXCUSES YOU TELL YOURSELF: MONEY

I can always return it.

———◆———

If I didn't spend a hundred dollars,
I couldn't get the free gift!

———◆———

Shopping is good for the economy.
I'm just doing my part.

———◆———

They offered me interest-free financing.

———◆———

That's what credit cards are for.

———◆———

The kids can't go to school
dressed like paupers, can they?

I had a coupon.

It was on sale.

I had a coupon and it was on sale.

It's an early birthday present.

I just got my tax refund.

But it's the last one!

The Smiths have three of them!

I deserve it.

It's one of a kind!

It will only appreciate in value.

You have to spend money to make money.

I'll stop going out to dinner and buying lattes and I'll bring my lunch every day.

But it makes me feel so good.

I can write it off.

It's cheaper than surgery.

It's cheaper than therapy.

BAD BEHAVIOR: CUTTING IN LINE

I asked some guy to hold my place.
Where did he go?

———————◆———————

This is an express lane? I didn't realize.

———————◆———————

I was actually here before you.

———————◆———————

My five different flavors of ice cream and
my three liters of diet soda really count
as just two items.

———————◆———————

You're shopping for a whole battalion
and I just have this little basket.

———————◆———————

I'm an anarchist; I don't believe in organization.

I think I'm going to throw up.

You turned around to look at a magazine
and lost your place in line.

I have a sick puppy at home.

I have a sick child at home.

BAD BEHAVIOR:
RETURNING GOODS

It was broken when I got it.

It smelled like this when I got it.

It didn't have tags when I bought it.

What kinds of dorks keep their receipts?

———◆———

I had to open it to discover that I didn't want it!

———◆———

I had to tear up the receipt so my husband
wouldn't see how much it cost.

———◆———

My dog ate my receipt.

———◆———

It was a gift from my dying grandmother.

BAD BEHAVIOR:
UNPAID BILLS

The check is in the mail.

———◆———

Well, then the post office must have lost it.

FAKE IT 'TILL YOU MAKE IT

Whether it's "I'll quit tomorrow" or "I deserve those shoes," spurious thoughts may help you achieve success. Books like The Secret dubiously recycle the concept of positive thinking, dubbing it the "law of attraction" or "intentionality"—if you think it, it will come—but there's some neurological data to back that up. Further, studies have shown that happy people are less honest with themselves than depressives, just one more reason to self-deceive.

I forgot to sign it? My stars,
I'll send you another one right away.

───◆───

The bill-payer in this household
isn't here right now.

I thought all utilities accepted bitcoin.

Somebody in your office
gave me the wrong address.

Someone must have accidentally
thrown that bill away.

I didn't really even watch cable this month.

That bill was really confusing.

Clearly, it's identity theft.

I ended that service months ago.

I forgot to carry the zero.

BAD BEHAVIOR:
MOTOR MISHAPS

The tree came out of nowhere.

———◆———

That yellow did not last
the legally required duration.

———◆———

The sun was in my eyes.

———◆———

That pedestrian totally ran into my vehicle.

———◆———

It all happened in an instant when I sneezed.

———◆———

There was a bee in the car.

———◆———

I was just going with the flow of traffic.

REJECTIONS

— *Preparing to Approach the Inevitable* —

At some moment in every person's life, it will be necessary to deliver a breakup or rejection. For most of us, however, these unpleasant occurrences arise with reasonable frequency, whether firing someone, quitting a job, telling a therapist he doesn't understand human nature, delivering news of inadequacy, turning down a pickup attempt or breaking up with a lover, or terminating a dysfunctional relationship with a family member, friend, or pet. The anxiety induced by these situations is among the highest we will face in our jobs and personal lives. Most people lose sleep before dropping the ax, mentally rehearsing how the scene will play out. Those whose fear prevents them from making necessary changes will live diminished lives as they are increasingly surrounded by people who bring them down.

While no guide can alleviate the need to confront an unworkable situation and the person behind it, this chapter arms you with scripts to end any relationship. Many books address the challenges of being on the other side of the equation—the one who is fired or dumped—but few tackle the equally distressing position of the one doing the dirty work. Now, you'll never again be left without the right words.

When choosing your lines, think about your delivery style: Droll? Dry? To the point? Via text? Cruel? Also consider your relationship with the about-to-be-terminated. Is it an intimate? An acquaintance? Professional or personal? Have they done something truly wrong, such as lie or steal? Next, formulate your desired outcome, both short- and long-term. While it's all-too-tempting to say "Go to hell," such definitive or insulting approaches may come back to haunt you. Life is short and memories are long, so be absolutely certain that the bridge you burn is a bridge you will never again want to cross.

So many of us have put off difficult encounters. Now, however, you hold in your hands the solution to your problems, your own personal Cyrano de Bergerac. No matter the situation, person, or pet, you'll feel powerful and in control with this panoply of witty, effective lines.

"We're not astrologically compatible."

YOU'RE FIRED

Let's go talk outside.

———◆———

We want to wish you luck
in your future endeavors.

———◆———

Here's your paycheck.
You may notice it's pink.

———◆———

This is as hard for me to say
as it is for you to hear.

———◆———

Some day soon you may want to
use me as a reference.

———◆———

These are the days I hate being a boss,
but I won't be your boss much longer.

I share your pain, though
technically I've never been fired.

We'll both be happier when you're free
to pursue your other interests.

Good news! You get to file for unemployment!

Here's a box for your personal belongings.

You will be missed.

Don't think of this as a closed door;
look at it as an open window.

I'd like to take a minute to go over
your severance package.

We have a zero-tolerance policy for morons.

Start looking in your mailbox
for your final check.

———◆———

You can drink all day now if you want.

———◆———

It's just not working out.

———◆———

Don't look at it as losing
a job—look at it as regaining a life.

———◆———

Before I go any further, I'd like to offer
you the opportunity to resign.

We don't look at it as downsizing—we look
at it as rightsizing.

———————◆———————

Consider this your final job evaluation:
Termination Effective Today.

———————◆———————

Management says we have to trim some fat.

———————◆———————

There's no room for you on our new
organizational chart.

———————◆———————

Welcome to Outplacement Training.

———————◆———————

I'm sure you've heard the rumors
about the head count readjustment.

———————◆———————

The workforce agreement is no longer in force.

The views on your blog are contradictory to the values of our corporate culture.

Every failure needs a scapegoat.

You're being merged out,
effective yesterday.

TIP: WHEN TO FIRE

Experts disagree on the timing of employee termination. Some say you should fire in the first part of the week so the employee doesn't brood about it over the weekend and so other employees can address their concerns about the firing. Others recommend terminating late on a Friday so the employee can have some privacy and clear the premises discreetly. Ultimately, do it when you feel it's right. It's never going to be the right time for them, so why not make it easy on yourself?

Headquarters has mandated a paradigm shift,
and you're no longer paradigmatic.

———————◆———————

You just don't have the adequate bandwidth.

———————◆———————

We're delighted to be able to
offer you this career change opportunity.

———————◆———————

Waste expulsion happens.

———————◆———————

Quite frankly, you're subprime.

———————◆———————

Congratulations! You've been selected
to take the payout.

———————◆———————

There's no "i" in "team," and
there's no "u" in "employed here."

Your job is no longer future-proof.

———————◆———————

Hi! I'm your replacement.

———————◆———————

I'll make this short—today's your last day.

———————◆———————

I'm so sorry you won't be at
the company holiday party this year.

———————◆———————

Since you refuse to quit,
I have no choice but to fire you.

———————◆———————

IT will be helping you transfer all your company
files to the server before you leave today.

———————◆———————

This is your last chance to take advantage of the
employee discount, so you may want to stock up.

Don't feel bad—this is our fault. We should have never hired you in the first place.

———————◆———————

We're moving in a you-free direction.

———————◆———————

This isn't business, it's personal.

———————◆———————

We've decided to invest in the future rather than overcome the mistakes of the past.

———————◆———————

We've both failed. You failed to succeed, and I failed to fire you sooner.

———————◆———————

You're not part of the solution, you're part of the problem.

———————◆———————

We've found a machine that can do your job better.

Your personality doesn't serve
you well in the workplace.

———————♦———————

These security guards are going to
escort you out of the building.

I QUIT

I want to go out while I'm still
at the top of my game.

———————♦———————

This is the best job I've ever had;
I know it'll be downhill from here.

———————♦———————

You will always be the gold standard of bosses.

———————♦———————

Poverty will be easier than working for you.

———————♦———————

I've decided to go back to school—full-time.

I believe you deserve someone
who's 100 percent committed.

I look forward to training my replacement.

I was meant for bigger things.

I always thought I'd be a working mother, and I
appreciate your holding my job open for me and
paying high-level temps during my six-month
maternity leave, but now that the baby's here,
my priorities have changed.

I've learned so much from you that it's
time to start my own business.

Though this job has been financially and
emotionally rewarding, I can no longer
deny my dreams.

I've decided to be independently wealthy.

———◆———

It's my goal to have a dozen careers
by the time I'm fifty.

———◆———

I'm dropping out of the rat race.

———◆———

I've decided to go freelance.

———◆———

I had a vision—it's not this.

———◆———

I just keep wondering, "What's it all for?"

———◆———

Though I've learned some valuable things
about human nature, I want to leave while
I still have some dignity.

If you give me a year's severance pay,
I promise not to testify against you.

I'm the corporate leak.

I'm going to miss our Saturday morning
meetings and midnight conference calls.

STILL ROYALTY-FREE

In 2004, Donald Trump attempted to trademark
the phrase "You're fired!" (both with and without
the exclamation point), which he had popularized
in his television show, *The Apprentice*. He faced
opposition from a small ceramics store in Illinois
that had previously filed to trademark the phrase
as well as from the makers of the educational
board game "You're Hired!" Trump's application
was denied.

I've accepted a position that
doesn't require me to wear a uniform.

I never meant to stay this
long in the first place.

I'm losing my identity in our corporate image.

I don't want to go down with this ship.

I haven't forgotten about company loyalty. I've
just chosen to be loyal to another company.

This job isn't exactly the
gold mine you promised.

I've got a concussion from the glass ceiling.

While I can honestly say I've learned a great deal from this experience, you can pick up your own damn dry cleaning from now on.

I'm too old for this crap.

I've just made my last pot of coffee.

I'm really a creative!

Although it's a thrill to see my ideas implemented, it's no longer fun watching you get all the credit.

Here's my resignation. Now you can't fire me.

I refuse to continue covering for your incompetence.

The truth is I quit doing this job six months ago. I've just been showing up to collect a check and the bennies.

———◆———

I can't work for a boss who doesn't understand my genius.

———◆———

I have so much more to offer.

———◆———

My doctor said I should quit.

———◆———

My therapist said I should quit.

———◆———

Thanks to you, my self-esteem has never been lower.

———◆———

I hope we can still be friends.

I'm just a number to you.

LETTING GO OF
A THERAPIST

The voices in my head are
telling me to get a new therapist.

———————◆———————

I can analyze my own dreams.

———————◆———————

I always leave feeling worse than when I came in.

———————◆———————

The fifty-minute hour is an oxymoron.

———————◆———————

You say I need to move away from denial, but
what if I'm in denial about being in denial?

DON'T QUIT—GET FIRED

While it's extremely gratifying to quit your job, it may be more financially beneficial to get yourself fired. Termination without cause will reap you unemployment and, if you play it right, severance pay. Cause-free self-sabotage can be tricky, however, so tread carefully. Start by extending your lunch breaks and getting sick a lot. Escalate to turning in sloppy reports, misunderstanding directions, and moping around.

I'm not getting sane fast enough.

My obsession with you has cooled.

Your couch is lumpy.

I've decided to go down the path of self-help.

We just keep going over and
over the same ground

You've empowered me enough to say,
"I'm never coming back."

LETTING GO OF
A DOCTOR

You don't validate for parking.

I've found another doctor who will
give me pain medication on demand.

No matter how many times I get sick,
you still think I'm a hypochondriac.

It appears that you skipped the
bedside-manner class in medical school.

I found a second opinion I liked better.

I got a second opinion and
they agreed you're a lousy doctor.

You always insist on weighing me.

LETTING GO OF A DENTIST

You get so jumpy when I bite you.

You have such a fetish about flossing.

You charge too much for nitrous.

You're so down in the mouth.

LETTING GO OF A HOUSEKEEPER

I know you saw what I did.

———◆———

You're just not skilled
enough at stain removal.

———◆———

You're too chatty.

———◆———

You found my secret stash.

———◆———

The house didn't pass the "white-glove" test.

———◆———

By using the no-clutter method, I've gotten rid
of all those material things that don't spark joy.
Turns out, that's what you were cleaning.

LETTING GO OF A GARDENER

I bought my own lawn mower.

We're putting in a rock garden.

We're turning our backyard
into a basketball court.

I thought you had a green thumb,
but I see now it's just mold.

Our garden is so overgrown that
our dog got lost for two weeks.

We're spending too much on the
housekeeper to afford a gardener.

LETTING GO OF
A POOL CLEANER

I got an acid burn in the Jacuzzi.

———◆———

I can't see the bottom.

———◆———

We're draining the swimming pool
for the next few winters.

———◆———

We've purchased a
mechanical pool sweeper.

———◆———

We're turning our pool
into a composting area.

———◆———

I hired a service who will
do the same thing for less money.

LETTING GO OF
A HAIRDRESSER

The look I was going for
was not "meth addict."

———————◆———————

You just don't understand my hair.

———————◆———————

Your personal style doesn't inspire
enough confidence for me.

———————◆———————

I still haven't recovered emotionally
from the last haircut.

———————◆———————

I don't think my face shape
is suited to the mullet.

———————◆———————

I'm shaving my head.

CHANNELING MRS. BEETON

In 1861, Isabella Beeton, Martha Stewart's Victorian predecessor, published the definitive and charmingly exhaustive *Mrs. Beeton's Book of Household Management*. Apply her terminology as cause for discharging your household help, including "Sad want of elbow-grease," "Creaking of shoes an abomination," or "Not to . . . offer any opinion, unless asked for it; nor even to say 'good night' or 'good morning,' except in reply to that salutation."

LETTING GO OF A MASSAGE THERAPIST

I asked for Swedish, you gave me
Shiatsu—in my book, that's unforgivable.

Smooth jazz is for sissies.

I wanted a massage;
I didn't want you to play Whac-A-Mole.

It turns out I'm ticklish.

My doctor told me
I'm incapable of relaxing.

I got a massage chair for Christmas.

Your hands are cold.

Last time I was covered
in bruises the next day.

I really just wanted the happy ending.

LETTING GO OF
A PERSONAL TRAINER

I just can't work out with
someone who's as fit as you are.

———◆———

My abs aren't responding the way I'd hoped.

———◆———

You're too critical of my downward dog.

———◆———

If I wanted to be abused,
I'd visit my family more often.

———◆———

I've reached my goal—acceptance
of my body the way it is.

———◆———

I just remembered that vanity is a sin.

I liked your approach. Now let's see your departure.

LETTING GO OF
A CHILDCARE PROVIDER

The nannycam results are not good.

———◆———

My friend's nanny said she saw you giving
the children non-organic food at the park.

———◆———

Your bedtime stories
are scaring the children.

———◆———

I don't know where else my toddler
would have learned to swear.

The children have started
calling you mommy.

———————◆———————

My husband mumbles
your name in his sleep.

LETTING GO OF
A DOG WALKER

My neighbor said she saw you
let the dog off the leash.

———————◆———————

My neighbor said she saw
you fail to pick up after my dog.

———————◆———————

My neighbor said you
spoke harshly to my dog.

———————◆———————

My neighbor said you walk really slowly.

My neighbor said that the dog walks
you more than you walk the dog.

My neighbor said the dog looks really unhappy.

My neighbor said she'd walk the dog.

TIP: DO IT IN PERSON

While it may be tempting to terminate an employee via remote or electronic means, it's definitely the cowardly way out and will not be looked upon kindly. In 2006, RadioShack was vilified in the press for firing four hundred workers by email. They dug the hole deeper by using unclear corporatespeak: "The workforce reduction notification is currently in progress. Unfortunately your position is one that has been eliminated."

CRUSHING DREAMS

You might want to try
community college first.

———◆———

There are so many good jobs
available to high school graduates.

———◆———

Your definition of "extracurricular"
differs somewhat from ours.

———◆———

As expressed in your college application essay,
your life has been too easy.

———◆———

You can't afford our tuition, but your parents
make too much to receive financial aid.

———◆———

We can't take a chance on a job-hopper.

The virus attached to your
resumé crashed our server.

———◆———

Your Facebook page indicates that
you're not ready for a real job.

———◆———

Your background check
showed some irregularities.

———◆———

Your quoted objective, though entertaining,
reveals a lack of direction.

———◆———

When you're an hour late for
the interview, you can't expect much.

———◆———

Your salary expectations are completely out of
line with your skill set and past experience.

We'll keep you on file should a future
opportunity present itself.

———————◆———————

You spent the entire interview bad-mouthing
your previous employers.

———————◆———————

With all that you have going on,
I don't think you could handle this job.

———————◆———————

We spell-checked and fact-checked your
résumé—clearly, someone had to.

———————◆———————

Though your references are glowing,
your résumé flawless, and your interview skills
exemplary, we've decided to hire someone else.

———————◆———————

You're completely
overqualified for the position.

ACTING REJECTIONS

We need someone a little less urban.

———————◆———————

We need someone a little more ethnic.

———————◆———————

We're looking for someone a little younger.

———————◆———————

We're looking for someone a little older.

———————◆———————

We're looking for someone a little better looking.

———————◆———————

We're looking for someone a little more real.

———————◆———————

We need someone who can dance.

———————◆———————

We need someone who can sing.

We need someone who can act.

You just don't have "it."

Don't quit your day job.

WRITING REJECTIONS

The writing lacks style and the content lacks interest. However, the spelling is impeccable.

Your author photo wouldn't be marketable.

I fell asleep by the tenth page.

We could reconsider your work at a later date, but it will definitely be an uphill battle.

I've read this before—by somebody else.

I don't feel anything truly fresh here.

I think we can both agree
it's not your best work.

You'd be better served by an editor who's
passionate about your work.

Your autobiography just doesn't ring true.

The funniest parts of your
book are the grammar errors.

It's just not what we're looking for—nor,
I fear, is anyone else.

MAKE UP OR BREAK UP

When you try to open your heart to love, chances are you'll lose. One-third of us have been through a breakup in the past ten years. Half of first marriages and sixty percent of remarriages move on to divorce court. But there's still reason for optimism—since singles decide quickly (men, fifteen minutes; women, one hour) if someone is worth a second date, you can use the lines in this chapter to speed up your turnover rate.

ART REJECTIONS

Your style is derivative and your framing
decisions unfortunate.

⬥

Just because you're self-taught
doesn't mean it's outsider art.

⬥

Your work falls outside the arbitrary
parameters this gallery has established.

⬥

It's not really a stand-alone piece.

⬥

It just doesn't move anybody here,
except in the wrong way.

⬥

You're a premodern artist in a
postmodern world.

It's not quite gallery-quality.

The intended dialectic mines the semiotics of postexpressionistic symbolism, but it sucks nonetheless.

A picture may indeed paint a thousand words, but this doesn't say anything.

It's crap. No, really—it's crap.

PICKUP PUT-DOWNS

Has that line ever worked?

Sorry—I don't date outside my species.

Didn't you hit on me last night?

Yes, I come here often.
But I don't think I will anymore.

I'd like to help you out—which
way did you come in?

Sorry, I don't date people
who try to pick me up.

I don't have a phone.

Do I have to spell it out for you? N-O.

I'm not here to meet anyone.

I know you want to get into my pants,
but there's already one asshole in there.

Next.

I was winking at someone else.

I'd only be going out with you to
make my ex jealous.

You're geographically undesirable—actually,
just generally undesirable.

No need to go further—I already Googled you.

Don't make me get out my pepper spray.

You're nice—too nice.

THE ART OF REJECTION

Individual reactions to art are notoriously subjective. Whether to declare a work a masterpiece or a piece of garbage can feel completely arbitrary, but with Contemporary Art Gallery magazine's list of most frequently cited reasons for gallery rejection, you have plenty to choose from: style, quality, similarity, dissimilarity, low pricing, high pricing, location, logistics and administration, personality clashes, and gallery cliques.

Dogs are great judges of character,
and mine doesn't like you.

―――――◆―――――

We're not astrologically compatible.

―――――◆―――――

I'm really busy for the next few years.

My beer goggles fell off.

What could possibly have made you
think I would go out with you?

Aren't you gay?

BREAKUPS

I've grown too far beyond you.

It's not fair to you for me to stay.

My career is more important
to me than anything.

You're more in love with me
than I am with you.

You don't rock my world.

———◆———

I'm just not that into you.

———◆———

We're just at different points in our lives.

———◆———

My therapist told me we should break up.

———◆———

It's funny—I don't even want to be friends.

———◆———

I need to discover who I am without you.

———◆———

I think I might be gay.

———◆———

I think I might be straight.

I think you might be gay.

———◆———

I think you might be straight.

———◆———

You're way out of my league.

———◆———

I love you but I'm not in love with you.

———◆———

I woke up beside you and knew it was wrong.

———◆———

I can't forgive myself for cheating.

———◆———

I'm in love with somebody else.

———◆———

I want more sex. With more people.

You just don't "get" me.

———————◆———————

I'm not sure I ever loved you.

———————◆———————

It's not you, it's me.

———————◆———————

My mother says I deserve much better than you.

———————◆———————

Sorry, you're just not "the one."

———————◆———————

So many things that were cute
in the beginning now get on my nerves.

———————◆———————

You're not the same person I fell in love with.

———————◆———————

I hate your family.

I hate your friends.

I hate you.

You're a lying, cheating snake.
For some reason, that bothers me.

It's not me, it's you.

PROPOSAL REJECTIONS

No thanks.

What difference would a piece of paper make?

I'm just so happy with things
the way they are.

That's such a huge commitment.

———◆———

Don't you think it's a little soon?

———◆———

But I'm not pregnant!

———◆———

Why fix what ain't broken?

———◆———

You do realize that nearly half of
all marriages end in divorce, right?

———◆———

I don't believe in the institution of marriage.

———◆———

I've been meaning to tell you
that I think we should end things.

TIP:
THE MODERN BREAKUP

Because technology has made so many things easier, it's tempting to utilize it to deliver bad romantic news. Text messaging is best reserved only for the most casual of rejections. Email and voicemail avoid confrontation but could create fury on the other end. For any relationship of longer than a month, face-to-face is the only appropriate means. And using emojis during any breakup? Never recommended.

I don't see us growing old together.

You're not marriage material.

When I think of us, the word
"forever" just doesn't spring to mind.

What a surprise! If you really knew me,
you'd know that I hate surprises.

Is this a joke?

You call that a ring?

ENDING THE MARRIAGE

Let's end this before death does us part.

We got married for all the right reasons, but
we're staying together for all the wrong ones.

Marriage just isn't as fun as the wedding.

Nothing is unconditional.

I've come to know you better than anyone,
and I've realized I don't actually like you.

I've been faking it since the honeymoon.

I think it's time we call it a day.

I can't live with a morning person.

I don't want to waste
any more of my life on you.

It's time for me to upgrade.

The party's over.

MIND GAMES

— *Preparing to Play the Puppetmaster* —

Call it Machiavellian mind-gaming or mere finesse—most effective communication is manipulative, even when honest and well-intended. In fact, all communication between people may be seen as a form of jockeying, since it is almost always meant to affect the recipient and elicit a desired outcome.

In a world where mind games and guilt trips are standard operating procedure, what's a decent human animal to do? If one fights the system, one runs the risk of upsetting the social order, which can only lead to general mayhem and destruction. The key is not to refuse to play the game but to play it consciously, always staying honest with oneself—if not with others.

This chapter contains all you need to start manipulating people's heads and hearts with self-awareness and purpose—or, if you're already a pro, to improve your game. Are you wondering how exactly to use this chapter? Look at the headers for your clues—they'll give you all the categories you need to begin mentally freaking out the unsuspecting. For instance, we all know that guilt trips can be the mainstay of any familial relationship, and it turns out mind games are no different. Consider that parents are hardwired to manipulate children to protect both their safety and innocence. (What is Santa if not the ultimate mind game?) By providing a comprehensive variety of situations and relationships, this volume offers assistance not only to those already comfortable with the manipulative arts, but also to those new to the concept.

For everyone who lives in the real world, this chapter offers a wealth of verbal ammunition. On any given day, one is certain to face troublesome personalities who require a bit of wrangling, for their own good as well as yours. Your interactions will leave people feeling unsettled, slightly insecure, but uncertain why. This can only serve to improve your standing. As you learn to put people in their place, you'll gradually build an aura of personal mastery—all through the sport of emotional subterfuge. Let the mind games begin.

"I feel like I'm moving in a you-free direction."

TO CHILDREN

You have a different kind of beauty.

———◆———

Some people are just late bloomers.

———◆———

It's nice to see you didn't succumb to the
pressure to measure up to your brother.

———◆———

I'm just so happy I can be in a position to help.

———◆———

After all I've done for you...

———◆———

After all I've done for you...
and here it is, itemized.

———◆———

Think of all those starving kids in Africa.

I'm not mad, I'm just disappointed.

All you needed was a little push.

I just don't think that friend has
your best interests in mind.

You always were such a unique kid.

I can't expect all my
children to turn out well.

You're the best thing I've ever done with
my life. Promise you'll do better than I did.

An A-minus?

Don't you want to be popular?

You're the reason I'm still working.

———◆———

I'm not judging you. I hear people are waiting longer and longer to find the right partner.

———◆———

Most of you children were planned.

———◆———

Too bad you're doomed to grow up just like me.

———◆———

It's your life.

———◆———

You'll lose weight when you're really ready to try hard.

Make me proud!

Santa doesn't bring toys to naughty children.

If you keep screaming like that, the Easter Bunny
won't bring you any more candy.

If you don't believe in the Tooth Fairy,
the Tooth Fairy won't believe in you.

Isn't it wonderful that long-distance
calls don't cost a dime these days?

I'm only a short plane ride away.

Did you hear about the Anderson boy?
Right out of Harvard into a six-figure job!
His parents must be so proud.

CAUTIONARY TALES

Reading to your children at bedtime may turn out to have unexpected benefits. Fairy tales have long spooked children into submission with the most intimidating weapon of all: consequences. The classics provide explicit fates for naughty little boys and girls—just think of Goldilocks, Hansel and Gretel, and Little Red Riding Hood. Who wouldn't be cowed by angry, feral carnivores, a blemish-covered hag, or a depraved, cross-dressing wolf?

Birthday-schmirthday… it's thinking
of me at all that counts.

———————◆———————

I know you're too busy to come visit me;
of course your work should come first.

———————◆———————

All those great parties I missed can't compare
to the nights I spent at home changing your
poopy diapers.

———————◆———————

Don't even think about it—my heart only
stopped beating for a few short hours.

———————◆———————

I knew you'd be too busy,
so I already asked the neighbor.

———————◆———————

Not everyone gets to work doing what they
love instead of making a living.

This hurts me way more than it'll hurt you.

———————◆———————

I brought you into this world—and I can take
you out of it.

———————◆———————

It's fine.

———————◆———————

Is that what you're wearing?

TO PARENTS

You're right, it's better that I prepare
for college than have a real childhood.

———————◆———————

I can't blame all of my problems
on my childhood. But...

———————◆———————

I talk about you a lot—in therapy.

Your strong tiger-mom ways taught me
how to avoid developing a real sense of self.

———————◆———————

I could always call Child Protective Services.

———————◆———————

Don't worry. Nobody seems to notice the
effects of my being dropped as a baby.

———————◆———————

You didn't spend that money on my college
education just for me to take the first steady job
that comes around, did you?

———————◆———————

My crappy childhood made
me a stronger adult.

———————◆———————

Thanks again for the one time you listened
to me—when I didn't want those braces
back in sixth grade.

No problem, Mom, I don't expect you
to remember I'm allergic to nuts.

———————◆———————

I guess I'll wait till the ninth day
of Hanukkah for my present.

———————◆———————

Your food is so good when it isn't burnt.

———————◆———————

You and Mom helped teach me that
there really is someone for everyone.

———————◆———————

It's all the things you didn't do for me that made
me the part-time Walmart greeter I am today.

———————◆———————

Janie's parents are cool.

———————◆———————

None of the other parents are going.

People raise children differently now.

———————◆———————

You were so young when you had me—of course
you didn't know how to parent.

———————◆———————

Is that what you're wearing?

TO SIBLINGS

I'm telling.

———————◆———————

The only crappy thing of yours not
handed down to me was your diapers.

———————◆———————

I guess our parents knew
you needed the extra attention.

———————◆———————

You know you were adopted, right?

Mom loves you the most, but she likes me better.

———————◆———————

I know it's hard being the black sheep.

———————◆———————

Boy, you really remind me of Mom sometimes.

———————◆———————

Boy, you really remind me of Dad sometimes.

———————◆———————

I know that despite everything, Mom and Dad
tried their best with you.

———————◆———————

At least our parents have
one kid who makes them proud.

———————◆———————

Mom and Dad had to pay to get you friends.

I'm the cute one. You're the…"quirky" one.

You're so lucky I went through it all first.

I was here first.

MARRIAGE MIND CONTROL

Do all relationships involve a little mind control? In a *New York Times* column and subsequent book, Amy Sutherland explained how she applied animal training methods to her husband—rewarding good behavior, ignoring bad—successfully breaking him of irritating habits. Readers objected to her treating her husband like a dolphin, but there's no doubt that we all do this to make living with loved ones a little easier. Sutherland is just a lot more explicit about it.

TO SPOUSES

I'm sorry the kids are stressing you out.
They stressed me out too when they
were inside me for nine months.

———————◆———————

That dress is nice.
You'll be wearing a sweater, right?

———————◆———————

If you want, I can show you how to
change the trash bag tomorrow morning.

———————◆———————

Maybe you can try to do the dishes this month.

———————◆———————

If you loved me, you'd love my parents, too.

———————◆———————

It's not you; it's how you make me feel.

I'm sorry for being passive-aggressive.
I'll try to be more aggressive next time.

No, it's adorable how you shout "The
Freshmaker!" each and every time you flush.

Think of the children for once!

Is that what you're wearing?

PHYSICAL PROWESS

Sometimes one learns the most from losing badly.

It's not like I purposely set out to beat you.

Jeez, I just happened to be the much,
much quicker one today.

I did that too, when I first started.

———◆———

Anyone could have
missed that long, high fly ball.

———◆———

I usually only play tennis with
people who can really challenge me.

SUPERIORITY

Why don't we have the party at my house?
I have plenty of room.

———◆———

I don't like to say how much
it was—that's just gauche.

———◆———

It's a bit early for me, but you
go right ahead and have that beer.

If you loved me, you'd let me do that.

I hate going to these expensive benefits all the
time, but at least I get to wear that old tux.

———◆———

It's fantastic how you're getting
the most out of that old car.

———◆———

We paid so much for our second house,
we really try to use it whenever we can.

———◆———

That's such a cozy place you guys bought.

———◆———

I really dug them before they
signed with a major label.

I loved that director back
when he was cutting edge.

I prefer spending my time doing public service.

I'd love to be a moderate like you.
I guess I just care too much.

The beach sounds like fun. But I have
to escort women to Planned Parenthood
today—I know, boring, right?

I love the idea of living in the suburbs—but I'd
miss all the culture one finds in the city.

INTELLIGENCE

Where did you go to college?

Did you go to college?

I thought everyone knew that.

You're applying to
community colleges too, right?

ONE OF US!

Brainwashing, a term coined in 1950 by journalist Edward Hunter, lies at the extreme end of the mind game spectrum. From cults to Mao Zedong's Chinese prison camps, breaking someone down and rebuilding them is an art and a science. Isolate someone. Fill them with self-doubt. Make them eat and sleep on your schedule. Let them know you can save them. Repeat. Along the way, hope for your sake they don't go "Private Pyle" à la *Full Metal Jacket*.

If you don't understand, I can go over it again.

———◆———

That's an…interesting idea.
However did you think of it?

———◆———

I'm sure there are a lot of good jobs for people
with just a high school degree.

———◆———

You do read the *New York Times*, don't you?

FRIENDSHIP

We were just talking about you!

———◆———

I'm always here for you.

———◆———

I guess you guys were just too busy
to call when you were in town.

No worries, I look terrible in
a bridesmaid's dress anyway.

A text is almost as good as a thank-you note.

Who does that?

Sounds like you had a great time.
I would love to have been invited.

If I can't have my own baby, at least
I get to hear every detail about yours.

I think you've mistaken me for your psychologist.

I wish I could be as honest as you, but I try to
get along with everyone.

APPEARANCE

It would be so fun to give you a makeover!

———◆———

You must have a fantastic metabolism
the way you're putting away those carbs.

———◆———

I thought for sure it would look good on you.

———◆———

That's a much better haircut for you.

———◆———

Your orthodontist sure had
his work cut out for him!

———◆———

Have you been sick?

———◆———

Selfies are not your ideal medium.

You know, they have some wonderful
medication for skin problems now.

———————◆———————

I loved those shoes when they
came out two seasons ago.

———————◆———————

Sure, I'm good looking, but you're so funny.

———————◆———————

I love how you don't care
what people think.

———————◆———————

Gosh, you've filled out
nicely over the summer.

———————◆———————

I'm guessing you'll want seconds.

———————◆———————

You look good for your age.

GAME, SET, MATCH.

Whether you're on a sales call or a first date, here are two great ways to psychologically game the odds and seal the deal.

1. Don't talk too much. Studies have shown the most successful salespeople aren't the fast-talking smoothies, but those who combine both golden tongues with a willing ear.

2. Be a mimic. Strategic mimicry, or the ability to mirror your mark's body language makes you appear more empathetic.

ROOMIES

How come you never write
about me in your diary?

I'm sure you didn't intend
to give me your cold.

The water ring you left on the coffee table goes
perfectly with the stain you left on the couch.

———◆———

I just love the smell of
your fermenting kimchi.

———◆———

Hey, what's a toothbrush between
nearly complete strangers?

———◆———

It's really been a great education
meeting all your one-night stands.

THE PICKUP

I can tell you're not one of those frigid,
stuck-up, unadventurous types.

———◆———

I stare—because I care.

There's no need to get emotional.

You might as well start thinking about where you and I are going to have breakfast tomorrow morning.

———◆———

I can tell from the people you attract that you are, indeed, quite popular with a certain type.

———◆———

Those are awesome—they almost look real.

———◆———

How much did you pay for that nose?

———◆———

Nice smile—who did your veneers?

Oh! I thought you were gay!

I can do better.

Having met your brother,
I thought you'd be really hot.

Are people really attracted to that look?

You're okay with an
open relationship, right?

I'll call you.

I'll text you.

SEX

No, baby, threesomes are totally overrated.

———————◆———————

I almost never fake it with you.

———————◆———————

None of my previous
partners seemed to mind.

———————◆———————

That's okay, I know how much
getting off first means to you.

———————◆———————

Anything bigger would be too much.

———————◆———————

If you loved me,
you'd let me do that to you.

———————◆———————

Some people just need more practice.

The other girls loved that.

I used to be a prude, too.

How do I know if I climaxed?

Is it always over so quickly?

Hey, if that's what you're into…

That's okay. It happens to a lot of older men.

Are you sure you're ready for that?

Poorly endowed guys are usually better in bed.

Don't sweat it, I have a vibrator.

I only watch porn to learn
how to be better with you.

You might want to consider watching
some porn, you know, for ideas.

I think it would be sexier if we
keep the lights off and our clothes on.

Is it in?

Was that it?

Did you come?

TURN IT OFF

Music plays tricks on the mind. It can set the mood for impending doom—think *Jaws*; it can also be the doom itself, as employed by the US military. Torturous tunes condoned by the Bush Administration to torment and intimidate at Guantánamo Bay (and beyond) have a surprisingly diverse range—everything from Bruce Springsteen's "Born in the U.S.A." to the theme song from *Barney & Friends* have been played to deleterious effect.

That was so nice.

I'll call you.

I'll text you.

DATING

I told you from the beginning—I'm not
looking for anything serious.

I just flirt with other people
to give them a thrill.

"Postmodern feminist"—so that
means I'm paying tonight?

I think it's great that you still keep
in touch with all your ex-boyfriends.

If it's meant to be, it's meant to be.

Let's wait a little longer
before we call this a "date."

Let's not go anywhere too public.

Your Uber ride home will be my treat.

I've been hurt too many times to commit.

Living together will take the
thrill out of our relationship.

RELATIONSHIPS: THE GIVER

I'll do it if it makes you happy.

Go ahead—just think of it
as "our" bank account.

If you leave me, I don't know what I'll do.

I think there might be something wrong
with your phone. I texted "I love you" and
I didn't get a response.

———————◆———————

I'm sorry for making you feel like you make
me apologize for too much, really, I am.

———————◆———————

I remember everything—it's okay if you don't.

———————◆———————

I want you to still be able to hang out with your
friends. Even the ones I think are a bad influence.

———————◆———————

Once we're married, I'm sure I can
undo your childhood damage.

———————◆———————

Don't worry about me—you should fulfill
your destiny while I put my silly little dreams
on hold for a little while.

RELATIONSHIPS:
THE TAKER

I should probably do all the
talking when you meet my parents.

———————◆———————

Other than that, my love is unconditional.

———————◆———————

I'd love to give you more attention,
but I need to take care of me first.

———————◆———————

Calm down!

———————◆———————

You're so sensitive!

———————◆———————

Practice being more confident.

———————◆———————

Thanks for doing this because you love me.

THE BREAKUP

We need to talk.

If I'm the one who's so selfish,
why are we still talking about your feelings?

There's no need to get emotional.

A PRINCE AMONG MEN

Oft misquoted (he didn't say, "the end justifies the means") and, perhaps, misunderstood, Niccolò di Bernardo dei Machiavelli nonetheless stands as the ultimate mind-gamer. Machiavellianism is "the view that politics is amoral and that any means however unscrupulous can justifiably be used in achieving political power," according to Merriam-Webster. Written in 1513, Machiavelli's *The Prince* formed the basis for his place as one of the founders of modern political science.

I have a certain image to live up to.

———◆———

I need to discover who
I am—without you.

———◆———

It's not fair to you for me to stay.

———◆———

You're too nice.

———◆———

I'm okay, you're okay—just not as much.

———◆———

I feel like I'm moving in
a you-free direction.

———◆———

Let me help you photoshop
your OkCupid profile picture.

PARENTING

I was just wondering if you knew
what comes after "spare the rod…"?

———— ◆ ————

Do you need some help
with your screaming toddler?

———— ◆ ————

Your kids' table manners are so—natural.

———— ◆ ————

I wish I could be as relaxed as you about
parenting, but I'm too much of a perfectionist.

———— ◆ ————

I'm sure your nanny is doing
a great job of raising your kids.

———— ◆ ————

I refused the epidural even though
I was in labor for 27 hours.

It took me a while to get
the hang of parenting, too.

———————◆———————

That's quite a shriek your kid has.

———————◆———————

I bet your child will be smart in other ways.

———————◆———————

I can see why those rock-band babyshirts are so
popular—they really show off your individuality
as parents.

A SOCIAL CONSCIENCE

So, what do you think your
carbon footprint is in that thing?

———————◆———————

What's one more degree of global warming,
more or less, when your car makes you look hot?

I'm sure your Hummer isn't
compensation for anything.

———◆———

She's beautiful. I'd get a purebred, too, if I could
live with myself for making that decision.

———◆———

Nice leather jacket.
I bet it looked almost as good on the cow.

———◆———

I hope your diamond is
fair trade and cruelty-free.

———◆———

If anybody can spend three long weeks
brewing a small batch of pure, handcrafted,
artisanal mustache wax from locally sourced,
freegan, recycled candles just to barter it for a
ten-ounce jar of hydroponically grown pickled
baby turnips, it's you, Thelonious.

Wow. That's a bold look.

So, do you find that your e-reader was worth the
local bookstore that went out of business for it?

My children attend public schools, of course.

I recycle, compost, and keep worms.

PERSONAL STYLE

Always keep in mind, dear: less is more.

Are you testing out your
Halloween costume already?

Those shoes are an interesting choice.

I must have missed hearing that
the unkempt look is in this season.

It can be so hard to tell the difference
between vintage and out-of-date.

I could never be as confident
as you are to have that haircut.

Is that what they call thrift-store chic?

It must be liberating to care so
little about your appearance.

Those pants really show off your ankles.

I hope you got a receipt for that.

TIP:
REPUTATIONAL CAPITAL

Make yourself a more convincing manipulator by garnering a reputation for following through on threats and intimidation. According to experts at the Harvard Business School, you only need to make good on an ultimatum once or twice to gain what is called "reputational capital," which proves that you're serious and lends credibility to all subsequent interactions, no matter how fake, empty, or outlandish. As a result, your weaker opponent will more than likely back down.

TO THE BOSS

I can't imagine how tired you must be
after a long day of bossing people around.

My ideas always sound so much
better when you take them.

I'd love to come to the meeting, but I assume
you want to be the smartest one in the room.

———◆———

Paying me in "valuable experience" is fine,
as long as you accept "imaginary work."

———◆———

It's my job to make you look
good—you really keep me busy.

———◆———

Did you know I won a
sexual harassment suit at my last job?

TO UNDERLINGS

How's about showing me your "A-game"?

———◆———

Plenty of people would
love to be in this position.

If you can't take the corporate heat,
stay out of the corporate kitchen.

Maybe you just don't want it enough.

This is really my fault—I knew
you weren't the right fit for this job.

I'd invite you to the meeting,
but this is an important client.

You've got a very bright future
ahead of you, somewhere.

How much of a raise do you think you deserve?

I'd hate to be disappointed by your work.

Need I remind you
you're in the big time now?

Annual reviews are just around the corner.

I've got my eye on you.

Have you ever thought
about changing careers?

We both failed. You failed to succeed,
and I failed to fire you sooner.

Do you have any idea how many
résumés I get every week?

Is this your best work?

TO COWORKERS

Whoops, sorry! I thought you were an intern.

It's always a pleasure to cover your ass.

Some of us actually work for a living.

It's such a shame that you put so
much work into your proposal.

You're not supposed to "lean in"
so much that you topple over.

You explained it almost as well as I would have.

I'm sure the boss will see how hard you tried.

Sounds like you're in a little over your head.

Don't worry—they probably won't
have a robot do that for a while.

It's true that hard work really can
help make up for a lack of talent.

STAY SUBLIMINAL

At least one savvy filmmaker knows the power of a mind game—would *The Exorcist* have been as chilling if director William Friedkin hadn't inserted frightening subliminal images into the film? Just a few frames of suggestive imagery is enough, Friedkin says, to create "a jolting effect...meant not to show something but to suggest." The technique works so well that he's used it in at least three of his films as a means to slip potentially shocking imagery past censors.

Your concept of "work attire" is very interesting.

———◆———

You're probably going to add more to that
before the presentation, so it's a good start.

———◆———

I hate when I get called out all
the time for being the top salesperson.

———◆———

If I win one more time,
it's going to get embarrassing.

———◆———

It's like I can't help but get promoted.

———◆———

FYI—they took a lot of
pictures at the holiday party.

———◆———

Is this difficult for you to understand?

No one is indispensable.

———◆———

You're right—you shouldn't have told me that.

———◆———

Oh, here's your résumé. I found it in the printer.

TO CUSTOMERS

I'd love your opinion on how to do my job.

———◆———

Yes, I personally set these prices high
to upset people.

———◆———

My mom gave me lots of practice
dealing with people like you.

———◆———

Why don't you try the
99-cent store down the street?

TO SERVICE PEOPLE

I understand if that's the best you can do.

———◆———

The pressure of not having a
corporate job must be so freeing.

———◆———

That was almost as good as when I
make it at home.

———◆———

May I have another gin and
tonic—with gin this time?

———◆———

Can I have your name, please? And the spelling?

———◆———

I'm sure your manager will be very interested in
hearing about the way I've been treated today.

PUT-DOWNS

Preparing to Offend in Style

It is a basic human drive to criticize, a need as essential as love and important as freedom. Everyone does it countless times a day—even you. This doesn't make you unkind; even the nicest people habitually practice social or professional critique. We complain to a mate while waiting in an unbearably slow checkout line. We express frustration with annoying acquaintances, or shout indignation at the TV news. Indeed, simple conversation and decision-making are impossible without critical thinking—which is often by necessity insulting to some entity, idea, or person.

Today, with the rise of the Internet and social media, everyone truly is a critic. Online commenting encourages us to spout opinions gratuitously and continuously, creating an environment in which the harshest voices attract the most attention. Like it or not, trading jabs is not only a handy skill, it's also a necessary survival tool. But what is often lost in this barbed atmosphere is the joy, élan, and pure panache displayed in zingers by great wits of the past.

PUT-
DOWNS

Anyone can toss off a lazy slur ("You fat pig"), but such digs are a dime a dozen, reflecting poorly on the speaker more than the recipient. What has lasting impact is the one-liner as pithy as it is witty (e.g., "I've had a perfectly wonderful evening. But this wasn't it," as Groucho Marx is said to have quipped while leaving a party thrown by a Beverly Hills socialite). A cutting bon mot justifies its undeniable unpleasantness with a gift of intellect or humor, leaving a trace of dignity in its wake. In fact, it is really a playful opening volley inviting a hearty riposte.

Cleverly taunting others is not merely a privilege to be enjoyed, but a liberty to be utilized lest it be silenced in this litigious and rancorous world. It is this chapter's intention to help you exercise that right with full confidence. Moreover, this chapter will help you toss clips with zestful enjoyment and best of all, style. In this way, you will help make the world a safer place not only for free speech, but for wit and good taste.

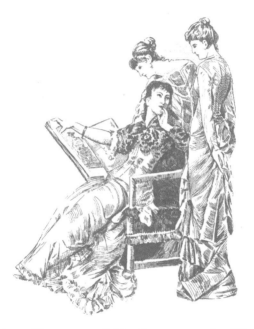

"I'm sorry—did I roll my eyes out loud?"

APPEARANCE

Are you what the cat dragged in?

———————◆———————

That really is a face only a mother could love.

———————◆———————

If that's not a mask, you should totally get one.

———————◆———————

You know what you'd look great in?
A full-body burlap sack.

———————◆———————

You're so ugly it hurts my feelings.

———————◆———————

Whoever gave you a "10" should
get back some change.

———————◆———————

Are you recycling those bags under your eyes?

Did it hurt when you fell from heaven? Because it looks like you landed on your face.

———————◆———————

Your picture is worth a thousand words, and all of them are synonyms for ugly.

———————◆———————

That baby is beautiful. Is she yours?

———————◆———————

Oh my God, look at you.
Was anyone else hurt in the accident?

———————◆———————

You must have your own ZIP code.

———————◆———————

Even your personality is ugly.

———————◆———————

I guess you're on the seafood diet:
you see food and then you eat it.

When you were born, the doctor screamed.

Inside every fat person is a skinny person
trying to get out. In your case, two.

It's good to see you.
Just not that much of you.

Your feet called. They miss seeing you.

You could stand to lose a few pounds.
On second thought, maybe you'd better sit.

Selfies aren't really your medium.

HYGIENE

Something's fishy—I'm guessing it's you.

———————◆———————

It wouldn't kill you to use deodorant,
but it might kill me if you don't.

———————◆———————

Did something die in your mouth?

———————◆———————

You draw more flies than
an entomological artist.

———————◆———————

I've smelled teenaged boys'
bedrooms that stink less than you.

———————◆———————

Please breathe the other way.
You're bleaching my hair.

AGE

Tell me more about the Paleolithic Era.

———◆———

You've had your face lifted so many times I'm
surprised there's anything left in your shoes.

———◆———

You're so old, Jesus owes you money.

———◆———

You're so old, you shouldn't
buy green bananas.

———◆———

Shouldn't you be at a bingo tournament?

———◆———

Many things improve with age.
You are not one of them.

———◆———

Your "get-up-and-go" has "got-up-and-went."

YOUTH

You don't know what we
did before the internet, do you?

If you drank from the fountain of youth,
you'd be a fetus.

I have boots older than you.

THESE WALLS CAN TALK

One-liners are an ancient art, as proven by graffiti discovered in Pompeii—a city frozen in ash from Mt. Vesuvius in AD 79. A few pithy Pompeiian epithets include: "Phileros is a eunuch," "Oh Chius, I hope that your ulcerous pustules reopen and burn even more than they did before," and "O wall, I am amazed that you have not fallen down since you support the loathsome scribblings of so many writers."

I'd invite you to dinner
but it's past your bedtime.

I'd slap you but I don't
want to be arrested for child abuse.

POOR STYLE

Are you in costume?

That's a one-of-a-kind piece—and there's a
reason no one else wanted it.

You're wearing that ironically, right?

The fashion police have a citation for you.

Money can't buy taste, can it?

Sorry, I couldn't hear you over your outfit.

———◆———

Was there a sale at Goodwill?

———◆———

It looks like you bought everything
you saw and wore everything you bought.

NUTS & CRAZIES

I don't have enough sandbags to
hold off the storm surge of your crazy.

———◆———

Your sanity left no forwarding address.

———◆———

You made a left turn at eccentric and
are heading straight toward batshit.

———◆———

When you chose your path, was it labeled socio?

Every one of your multiple
personalities thinks you're nuts.

———◆———

Too bad you're not the
entertaining kind of insane.

———◆———

You're not crazy like a fox—you're crazy
like a crazy person.

———◆———

Paranoid? I'll say. Everybody's
always getting together to talk
about how paranoid you are.

———◆———

If you were a number, you'd be irrational.

———◆———

You're the wonky bulb in
a string of Christmas lights.

CHEATS & LIARS

I met more interesting liars in kindergarten.

———————◆———————

You're in a dysfunctional
relationship with the truth.

———————◆———————

You need to get yourself some fireproof pants.

———————◆———————

Your ass must be jealous of all the crap that
comes out of your mouth.

———————◆———————

When it comes to sincerity, you're full of it.

———————◆———————

I didn't know snakes could
lie through their teeth.

———————◆———————

Do you wash both faces in the morning?

MULTICULTURAL MALIGNANCE

Slandering someone's brains or personality isn't always the most effective mode of insult, especially abroad. In Italy and Latin America, the surest means of offense is trashing a person's mother, while Dutch natives often mention disease or disability in their slams. In Arab regions, exposing the sole of your shoe is as offensive as it gets, while in East Asia, touching or patting someone on the head does the trick.

You inherited some good values,
but through diligent hard work,
you managed to overcome them.

———◆———

Do you believe anything you say?

———◆———

I'm sorry—did I roll my eyes out loud?

DUNDERHEADS

I'd insult you back,
but I don't think you'd get it.

———◆———

You spent twenty minutes looking at an orange
juice box because it said "concentrate."

———◆———

It takes you two hours to watch *60 Minutes*.

———◆———

Thanks for giving me a piece of your mind.
I know you don't have much to spare.

———◆———

If you had an "I'm with Stupid" shirt,
the arrow would just point up.

———◆———

You're as sharp as a very dull knife.

Did you already spend
all your common sense?

Great minds think alike, which explains
why we have nothing in common.

There's only one thing smaller than your
intellect, and I'm sure you don't want to
talk about that.

I'd jump into this conversation,
but I'm afraid I'd hit my head on the bottom.

PESSIMISTS

It's not everyone who can
find the bad in every situation.

Do you complain in your sleep?

You're a glass-totally-empty
kind of a person, aren't you?

I guess if you expect nothing,
you'll never be disappointed.

When life gives you lemons,
do you make funeral arrangements?

Any more whine out of you
and we could start a vineyard.

OPTIMISTS

Your ass must burn from
all the sunshine coming out of it.

Your enthusiasm is
infectious—like a disease.

A bad mood would be a
refreshing change for you.

———————◆———————

Your cup runneth over with oh my god shut up.

———————◆———————

Jiminy Cricket would get sick of your optimism.

BORES

Enough about you—let's talk
about something interesting.

———————◆———————

You're about as scintillating as a dial tone.

———————◆———————

Are you still talking? I fell asleep.

———————◆———————

I've seen wallpaper with more personality.

Please, go on. I always yawn when I'm interested.

Spending alone time with you makes me
wish I spent more time alone.

———◆———

It's not you, it's your personality.

———◆———

You should market yourself
as a cure for insomnia.

———◆———

You're almost as exciting
as a curling match.

———◆———

I admire your confidence in
assuming I give a shit.

LOSERS

You're not so much a
has-been as a never-will-be.

Someone has to be below average.

Do you have any achievements in real life?

The difference between
champ and chump is "u."

It's not everyone who can be
satisfied with mediocrity.

Everyone's good at something.
You're good at sucking at stuff.

VILIFYING THE HUBRISTIC

A truly pleonastic insulter will baffle and perplex pompous pseudo-intellectuals by using multisyllabic and arcane words to describe the cognoscitive inadequacies of others. Using as insults words like nescient, benighted, fatuitous, insensate, gormless, Boeotian, puerile, or oscitant has the double benefit of not only conveying their appropriate meaning, but also fortuitously making the insultee even more abashed by his ignorance of the term itself.

Should I send a search party
for your hidden talent?

Living in your parents' basement
would be a step up for you.

When I think of all the people I respect the
most, you're right there, serving them drinks.

ASSHOLES, EGOMANIACS
& NARCISSISTS

I think you're great,
but I'm a notoriously lousy judge of character.

◆

You must have great upper body strength from
climbing over all those people on your way up.

◆

At least you're not phony.
You want to be hated for who you really are.

◆

I wish I were as beautiful as you think you are.

◆

You should come with a trigger warning.

◆

How do you fit all that ego
in an average-sized body?

Let's play horse. I'll be the
front end and you be yourself.

———————◆———————

I'm looking forward to the pleasure of your
company—since I haven't had it yet.

HIPSTERS

Careful with that porkpie hat—after forty, you're
at greater risk of breaking your hipster.

———————◆———————

I bet you don't even need those glasses.

———————◆———————

I know you think you're unique, but you
look like everyone else in this dive bar.

———————◆———————

It must take forever to look
like you just rolled out of bed.

I wish I were as cool
as you think you are.

———◆———

I bet that tattoo is going to
look great in fifty years.

———◆———

Hipster.

PSEUDO-INTELLECTUALS

Doesn't your neck get tired
holding up that gigantic brain?

———◆———

Oh yeah, I read some
philosophy in college, too.

———◆———

Sartre was talking about you when
he said, "Hell is other people."

You can keep talking, but I won't keep listening.

I'm no expert, but neither are you.

ADDICTIVE TYPES

That much weed and you're still uptight?

Are you this stupid when you're sober?

Actually, you're not a fun drunk.

Friends accuse you of "acting weird"
whenever they meet you sober.

If I wanted someone to puke and fall on me,
I would have had kids.

TIP: "GOOD LUCK" IS BAD LUCK

It's always wise to insult a friend before a theatrical performance— in fact, artists around the world consider "good luck" to be akin to a curse. For actors, "break a leg" is the appropriate pre-curtain sentiment,  while dancers appreciate a hearty *merde* (French for excrement). Opera singers should be wished *toi toi toi* (an onomatopoetic phrase imitating the sound of spitting). And if your friend speaks Spanish, go with *mucha mierda* (lots of excrement).

IDEOLOGUES

Don't let the facts get in the
way of your opinions.

———————•———————

Does it get terribly hot in that cloak
of self-righteousness?

———————•———————

If ignorance is bliss, you should
be the happiest person alive.

———————•———————

You're so tight your ass squeaks.

SLACKERS & LAYABOUTS

If the secret to success is showing up,
you're doomed.

———————•———————

You make sloths look ambitious.

It's nice to know I can always
count on you to flake.

———◆———

Glaciers drag themselves across
the tundra faster than you.

———◆———

You're flakier than my grandmother's pie crust.

JERKS

I always forget the exact definition of
passive-aggressive. Thanks for the reminder.

———◆———

You don't need to be passive-aggressive
to get a rise out of me; your normal
personality does that just fine.

———◆———

Your passive-aggressive tendencies
go so well with your victim complex.

BETWEEN PARENTS & CHILDREN

Coming home to visit makes me
stronger—because it doesn't kill me.

You could be a great comfort in my old age,
if you weren't causing it.

Turns out, giving birth
to you was the easy part.

SIBLINGS

Mom sold you to the gypsies,
but they sent you back.

I wanted to get a pet lizard,
but Mom and Dad got you instead.

You're the sap in our family tree.

You were an accident.

Someone had to inherit the
crazy gene in our family.

Good thing Mom and Dad figured out
parenting by the time they got to me.

EXTENDED FAMILY

Spending time with you helps me
understand why my mom is so screwed up.

You're my favorite creepy uncle.

I look forward to your
oversharing every Christmas.

We're not losing a son; we're gaining a
controlling shrew.

We wanted our daughter to marry a kind,
intelligent person, but one out of two isn't bad.

This family has more nuts than a
squirrel with hoarding issues.

We don't complain about your shortcomings
but about your long stayings.

The difference between in-laws and
outlaws is that outlaws are wanted.

BAD FRIENDS

You're my best frenemy.

———◆———

I love when you cancel plans at the last minute—
it gives me more time to find new friends.

———◆———

Being your friend makes me feel
so much better about myself.

———◆———

Of all the people I've met you're
certainly one of them.

———◆———

You're unforgettable.
I keep trying to forget you exist.

———◆———

Now that I've gotten to know you,
I feel bad for your dog.

LOVERS

I'd rather pass a kidney stone
than another night with you.

There was something about you
that I liked, but you spent it.

You're not a bad lover, just…different.

TIP: DON'T LET THEM WIN

Posting online rants about companies' deplorable
customer service or defective products can provide
consumer catharsis, as well as a valuable warning
to others. Unfortunately, it may also push the
offending vendor's name higher in Internet search
results. Google is aware of this phenomenon and
has made efforts to revise its algorithms, but, for
now, it appears that there really is no such thing as
bad publicity—especially on the Internet.

LOTHARIOS & LECHES

Do you have a punch card at the free clinic?

I'm not your type. I'm not inflatable.

I totally want you—to go away.

You are validating my
inherent mistrust of strangers.

I'm not that desperate and
you're not that lucky.

With men like you in the world,
vibrator sales must be going up.

When you date a woman, do you arrive at the
door with flowers and antibiotics?

———◆———

Have you considered a career in sanitation?
You're great at picking up trash.

———◆———

I wouldn't even accept
your LinkedIn request.

———◆———

Sorry, I already have one ass in my pants;
I don't need two.

———◆———

Is it hot in here or
are you making me sick?

———◆———

I play softball, but I'm way out
of your league.

SLUTS &
ROMANTIC RIVALS

You've never met a man you
didn't like—for at least fifteen minutes.

———◆———

What's your favorite position—yes, absolutely?

———◆———

It may be time to
rediscover your inhibitions.

———◆———

I've heard you know how to say
"Where are my pants?" in seven languages.

———◆———

I don't like the word "slut," but
I'll make an exception for you.

———◆———

Guess you can't control your whoremoans.

BUREAUCRATS & PUBLIC AUTHORITIES

Did you go to remedial DMV-employee school?

———————◆———————

I'd call you a pompous ass
but I don't want to insult donkeys.

———————◆———————

Your attention to the details of this
job would impress Kafka.

———————◆———————

I thought "faceless bureaucrat" was just a saying.

———————◆———————

Which circle of hell do you
preside over in your spare time?

———————◆———————

If you ever leave your job in tech support you
could easily find work as a condescending turd.

A NEW (OLD) LOW

Every campaign season brings cries against vicious attack ads, but such tactics are nothing new. Thomas Paine called George Washington "the patron of the fraud," and papers labeled Abraham Lincoln "a fourth-rate lecturer." John Quincy Adams said Congressman John Randolph's "tongue drips poison"; Randolph in turn said Secretary of State Edward Livingston "shines and stinks like rotten mackerel by moonlight."

You've made great use of your fifteen minutes of customer-service training.

Do you practice your rude delivery or is it natural?

I got more useful customer service from your hold music.

You're like a used-car salesman
without the charm.

I'll take the #3—same as your IQ.

What number do I press to talk to a machine?

Did the city hire you because they don't
have to pay benefits to zombies?

What crimes did you commit
in a previous life to have this job?

Do you need training to be a court
officer, or just the shiny badge?

Could you move any more slowly?

COWORKERS

Failure is indeed an option
when I have to work with you.

———————◆———————

Thanks! Your crappy work makes me look great.

———————◆———————

Someone with your qualifications should
go far—and never come back.

———————◆———————

Do you save up all your lazy for the office?

———————◆———————

Can you teach me to be a better suck-up?

———————◆———————

Your brain is perpetually Out of Office.

———————◆———————

You have a black belt in brown-nosing.

OVERLINGS & UNDERLINGS

Do you deliberately base your
management style on the Spanish Inquisition?

It takes a true micro-intelligence to be
so good at micro-managing.

Saying you have a lousy work ethic
implies you have a work ethic.

What was I thinking when I hired you?

You put the ass in assistant.

Apparently there are stupid questions.

I just love covering for you.

LOUSY PARENTS

I can't wait to hear what your kid
says about you in therapy.

———————◆———————

Are you going to leash him?

———————◆———————

Did you know there are books on parenting?

———————◆———————

All babies are different—yours is just
really different.

———————◆———————

Cute kid. Is she feral?

———————◆———————

Maybe one day he'll run away from home.

———————◆———————

Have you considered installing
a GPS device on your kids?

Apparently there are stupid questions.

When did you get your helicopter license?

———————◆———————

Your children are so well-traveled.
They walk all over you.

———————◆———————

I've seen rabid raccoons with better
manners than your children.

———————◆———————

The endless stream of pictures you post
on social media about your children really
doesn't do them justice.

———————◆———————

Funny, one would think
parenting would be instinctive.

CITIZENS WITH POOR MANNERS

We'd all enjoy your phone conversation
if your life were remotely interesting.

———◆———

You can't cut in line—there's no room
for your giant sense of entitlement.

———◆———

Keep it down—everyone can hear
what an idiot you are.

———◆———

Were you born with a silver spoon up your butt?

———◆———

Just because you were born in a barn
doesn't mean you have to eat like a pig.

———◆———

Do you realize that people just tolerate you?

TIP: CINEMATIC SLAMS

If you find yourself at a loss for words, why not borrow from the silver screen? Here are some quirky classics:

- "Your mother was a hamster and your father smelled of elderberries!" —*Monty Python and the Holy Grail*

- "You are a sad, strange little man, and you have my pity." —*Toy Story*

- "There's a name for you ladies. But it isn't used in high society—outside of a kennel." —*The Women*

Whoever told you to be yourself
gave you terrible advice.

———◆———

I have neither the time nor the crayons
to explain to you how rude that was.

CELEBRITY CATCALLS

"I deny I ever said that actors are cattle. What I said was, 'Actors should be treated like cattle.'"
—Alfred Hitchcock

"I would trust her totally on cottage cheese."
—Restaurant critic Gael Greene,
on restaurant critic Mimi Sheraton

"He has never been known to use a word that might send a reader to the dictionary."
—William Faulkner, on Ernest Hemingway

"Poor Faulkner. Does he really think big emotions come from big words?"
—Ernest Hemingway, on William Faulkner

"Remarks are not literature."
—Gertrude Stein, on Ernest Hemingway

"Literary diarrhea."
—Noël Coward, on Gertrude Stein

———◆———

"They are so unbelievably horrible, so
appallingly unmusical, so dogmatically
insensitive to the magic of the art, that they
qualify as crowned heads of antimusic."
—William F. Buckley Jr., on the Beatles

———◆———

"Presumably, if you cannot be persuaded to read
anything better, Rowling will have to do."
—Harold Bloom, on J. K. Rowling's
Harry Potter and the Sorcerer's Stone

———◆———

"How does ... Francis Ford Coppola, one
of the greatest filmmakers of our time, see
Keanu Reeves's work, see what we've all seen,
and say, 'That's what I want in my movie'?"
—Charlie Sheen

"The last bit of methane left in the intestine of the dead cow that is post-modernism."
—Robert Hughes, on Jeff Koons

———————◆———————

"We don't need refs, but I guess white guys need something to do." —Charles Barkley

———————◆———————

"[Mamet's] ear has gone tone-deaf, and his social observations have devolved into clichés."
—Frank Rich, on David Mamet

———————◆———————

"Frank Rich and John Simon are the syphilis and gonorrhea of the theater." —David Mamet

———————◆———————

"I don't know about the siff, but a theatre without a clap or two would be a pretty lonely place."
—John Simon, in reply to Mamet's comment

"Every word she writes is false,
including 'and' and 'but.'"
—Mary McCarthy, on Lillian Hellman

"In fiction, she is a lady writer, a lady magazine
writer." —Lillian Hellman, on Mary McCarthy

"Somebody should clip Sting around the head
and tell him to stop singing in that ridiculous
Jamaican accent." —Elvis Costello

"The covers of this book are too far apart."
—Ambrose Bierce

"A professional amateur."
—Laurence Olivier, on Marilyn Monroe

"A bag of tattooed bones in a sequined slingshot."
—Mr. Blackwell, on Cher

"Who picks your clothes, Stevie Wonder?"
—Don Rickles, to David Letterman

"You don't take a sausage roll to a banquet."
—Winston Churchill, on why he would not
bring his wife on a trip to Paris.

HOMETOWN HARASSMENT

People often associate their personal identity with
the area in which they were born and raised. So
consider flinging the regional insult, which can
run from the macro to the micro:

- "America is a large, friendly dog in a very small
  room. Every time it wags its tail, it knocks over
  a chair." —Arnold Toynbee

- "California is a nice place to live—if you
  happen to be an orange." —Fred Allen

- "I love New York City. I've got a gun."
  —Charles Barkley

"We were trying to get pregnant,
but I forgot one of us had to have a penis."
—Roseanne Barr, on Tom Arnold

———————◆———————

"Bob is not authentic at all. He's a plagiarist, and
his name and voice are fake. Everything about
Bob is a deception. We are like night and day, he
and I." —Joni Mitchell, on Bob Dylan

———————◆———————

"The worst, most dangerous person to America
is clearly Paula Deen. She revels in unholy
connections with evil corporations…plus, her
food sucks." —Anthony Bourdain

———————◆———————

"The *g* is silent—the only thing about her that
is." —Julie Burchill, on Camille Paglia

———————◆———————

"Mr. Dean appears to be wearing my last year's
wardrobe and using my last year's talent."
—Marlon Brando, on James Dean

"Rock and roll is phony and false, and sung, written and played for the most part by cretinous goons." —Frank Sinatra

———————◆———————

"It amazes me how someone from your newspaper could ask such a stupid question." —Barney Frank, to Jennifer Steinhauer from the *New York Times*

———————◆———————

"If there's anything disgusting about the movie business, it's the whoredom of my peers." —Sean Penn

———————◆———————

"Rock journalism is people who can't write interviewing people who can't talk for people who can't read." —Frank Zappa

———————◆———————

"Don't be fooled by the dumb blonde routine. This woman is as smart as a rock." —Jimmy Kimmel, on Pamela Anderson

"Good for her. It's hard for little fat chicks to get anything going." —Howard Stern, on Lena Dunham and her TV show *Girls*.

"This person was just brought to my attention not too long ago. I'm not quite sure who this person is, to be honest. I don't know if it is a man or a woman."
—Christina Aguilera, on Lady Gaga

"It would be awful to be like Keith Richards. He's pathetic. It's like a monkey with arthritis trying to go on stage and look young."
—Elton John on the Rolling Stones band member

"And is that a great message for little girls? A whole family of women who take the faces they were born with as, like, a light suggestion?"
—Amy Schumer, on the women of the Kardashian family

COP-OUTS

Preparing to Rationalize

The truth hurts; in many situations it is best to avoid it entirely. Are you going to tell your brother that you can't come for Christmas because his wife is a grating shrew? Are you going to tell your stylist that she gave you the worst haircut ever? Are you going to tell your boss that the project is late because you stayed up all night rereading *The Stand*?

Because you never can tell when you're going to need them, we need to keep an arsenal of cop-outs and alibis at hand so that we can keep the peace, save our jobs and our relationships, and get out of seeing our friend's daughter attempt Sondheim. This chapter should do the less-than-truthful trick.

There's always the question of whether it's ethical to lie, even if it's harmless. (Not that cop-outs and alibis are always lies, per se. Often they're brilliantly calibrated truths delivered just so for maximum effect.) People who study this stuff agree: lies can help maintain relationships and make you feel better about yourself.

Since you can support most claims with some sort of evidence, we'll go with the experts who tell us lying can be good. (There's an alibi right there.) Researchers at the University of Toronto found that the skills you need to be a good liar—quick thinking and the ability to use information to your advantage—are signs of intelligence and predictors of success.

In this chapter, we give you guidance in a variety of situations to show off your intelligence and those social skills, covering your professional, personal, and public lives. We've got cop-outs for the workplace, your love life, and your relationships with friends and family. We also cover alibis you tell to people when you're out and about, and the special cop-outs you save for yourself.

George Washington, the very image of honesty, wrote, "It is better to offer no excuse than a bad one." We couldn't agree more. Bad excuses are a scourge upon our land. Use the cop-outs and alibis here and you'll have no excuse to use a bad excuse again.

"I'm too busy right now to date."

WORKPLACE LAZINESS

I was prepared for this meeting in a totally
unscripted, improv-comedy sort of way.

Napping at my desk is an inviolable
aspect of my Spanish siesta culture.

This is how they do it in the Teamsters.

I didn't write that proposal,
so I couldn't know we left that out.

I'm still waiting on a signature from purchasing.

I couldn't get enough buy-in, so I thought I'd
bring it up at our next staff meeting.

The client didn't respond to
my email asking for clarification.

———————◆———————

I can't do the team-building exercise.
I'm an introvert.

———————◆———————

Learning Excel wasn't
part of my vision board.

———————◆———————

I can't make people call me back.

———————◆———————

I would've worked on the pitch,
but I thought I was supposed to catch.

———————◆———————

I sent it from home, but forgot
we don't have Pages at the office.

The merger means there are certain redundancies.

I don't have the correct synergy
to envision those outcomes.

You're so much better at Power Point
presentations than I am.

I'm more of a big-picture person.

I had so much on my plate. You know, wearing
too many hats. I ran it up the flagpole to see who
would salute, but didn't get a hit on my ping.

Finding new ways to do nothing is the most
productive I've been all day.

BLAME TECHNOLOGY

I forgot the password. And my security question. And my mother's maiden name.

I can never figure out Excel.

I couldn't understand your emojis.

WASTE NOT...

In Salary.com's Wasting Time at Work 2014 survey, 89 percent of respondents admitted they waste work time daily. HR guru and venture capitalist Rudy Karsan likes to see workers switching between YouTube videos and work tasks: "When we start to do that we're really blending our lives together with work. I applaud it and hope we never lose that." So next time your boss sees you on Facebook, say you're improving your "work-life blend."

I was afraid you'd mistake the tone of my email
as passive-aggressive.

———————◆———————

It's just too technical—I'm not sure
you would understand.

———————◆———————

It got lost in the cloud.

———————◆———————

Someone took my flash drive.

———————◆———————

I have to wait for the social media feedback loop
to kick in before I can work on that any further.

———————◆———————

We're in beta testing and I really
can't say when we might be ready.

———————◆———————

I was going to work on that, but I'm waiting for
some feedback from our developers in India.

The IT team needs to install
an upgrade—it could be a while.

TARDINESS

My doctor insisted that I get more sleep.

Hackers broke into my alarm clock.

GIANT CLOWN, AGAIN?

The train from Cardiff to London delayed by a giant clown on the tracks? That's just one of the excuses offered in Britain for late trains. Other gems explaining service disruptions: signalman trapped in toilet, driver attacked by seagull, and dew on the tracks. The absurdity of the excuses has inspired a Twitter parody—TLF Travel Alerts— that posts excuses for delays and closures such as minotaurs, angry rat kings, and Earth Wizard and Fire Elf battles.

The ignition switch in
my car is under a recall.

———————◆———————

My therapist is encouraging me to
awaken to my own body clock.

———————◆———————

I have a "zero" passenger rating on Uber,
so I had to walk.

———————◆———————

I thought I saw a unicorn.

FIRING SOMEONE

You're so efficient that we've
run out of work for you.

———————◆———————

You're overqualified;
you make everyone else look bad.

We're holding you back in your career.

———— ◆ ————

You're a little too much of a team player.

———— ◆ ————

We're making a few cutbacks
in the "you" department.

———— ◆ ————

The company is doing well, other than
in its ability to pay its employees.

———— ◆ ————

The Chinese character for "crisis" is a
combination of those for "danger" and
"opportunity." What I mean to say is, we're
outsourcing your position to Beijing.

———— ◆ ————

We just couldn't find space
on the reorganized team.

It's our job to maximize profits for our
shareholders—so you have to go.

Think of the bright side—didn't you always say
you wanted to paint?

I'm afraid we are going to decline your
contract extension.

There's been a paradigm shift—away from you.

TO A MINION

I'd do it myself, but I have to
manage up—and that takes too much time.

You know, the go-getters in this
office stay late and help the team out.

It's just the corporate culture.

We need the private jet because
my time is just so damn valuable.

What can I say—crap rolls downhill.

I'll be sure to remember this when bonus time
comes around   next year.

OFFICE ETIQUETTE

Your lunch bag looks kind of like mine.

I was going to come back
and wash my mugs later.

The water bottle is too
heavy for me to switch out.

I meant to return your stapler, but someone
took it from me.

It's hard to tell which bin is for recyclables.

I was going to fill up the pot, but you're
so much better at making coffee than I am.

I was going to replace the paper in the copier,
but I couldn't find it.

CHEATING HEARTS
& OTHER PARTS

It wasn't a kiss—that's just
how the Inuit say hello.

I was just teaching him
how to properly tune a flute.

Sure, I was looking at her,
but I was thinking about you.

———— ◆ ————

You know how they spray you
with perfume at Bloomingdale's.

———— ◆ ————

Monogamy is so bourgeois.

———— ◆ ————

I didn't know we weren't seeing other people.

———— ◆ ————

Yes, it was a French kiss... because
he happens to be French.

———— ◆ ————

The heart wants what it wants. And so,
apparently, does my vagina.

———— ◆ ————

I was just trying to read the logo on her jeans.

We were discussing my previously unexpressed
passion for dentistry, one thing led to another,
and suddenly I'm inspecting her fillings.

———◆———

Open relationships are totally in.

———◆———

She came on to me and
I didn't want her feelings to get hurt.

———◆———

I went into that store to buy
you something sexy.

———◆———

I needed to learn more about
OkCupid for a story I'm writing.

———◆———

She was so drunk, I just wanted to
make sure she got to bed safely.

My phone was dead and I had a flat, so I went
into the strip club to use the phone to call AAA.

***

I thought we agreed out-of-town
conferences were fair game.

***

Shameless flirting is completely
acceptable behavior in Italy.

***

I meant to be "monogamous," but I
got it mixed up with "magnanimous."

GENERALLY BAD BEHAVIOR

If I compliment you too often
you'll get a big head.

***

I'm not the marrying kind.

I was preparing for a role;
it was method acting.

It's not that I wasn't paying attention to
what you were saying, it's that I was just
so distracted by your beauty.

I didn't say "I love you" because
words cheapen what I feel for you.

ESCHEWING RESPONSIBILITY

If I don't go drinking with the
guys I'll get left out of deals.

Valentine's Day is such a sexist, patriarchal
holiday I thought you'd appreciate staying in
and watching TV as a form of protest.

I left my wallet in my other pants.

My job is so stressful I just don't have the bandwidth to talk about feelings after work.

———◆———

This engagement ring doesn't have diamonds since I know how you feel about indigenous culture exploitation.

———◆———

I'd love to go to your second cousin's wedding, but you know how important that golf tournament is for client development.

———◆———

I would have walked Bootsy, but I could tell she missed you because you had to work twelve hours today.

DUMPING A DATE

The voices in my head say no.

———◆———

I took a vow of celibacy.

———◆———

I really don't want to
ruin our friendship.

———◆———

We're not astrologically compatible.

———◆———

Let's face it.
We're just not that into each other.

———◆———

I'm a lousy judge of character.

———◆———

You remind me of my dad.

IT'S ALL LATIN TO ME

Of Latin origin, the word "alibi" means "in or at another place." It was first used in the English language in legal contexts, to describe a plea that one was elsewhere when a crime was committed. It's worth noting that you usually can't introduce an alibi in the middle of a trial. In the US, while lawyers may keep their defense secret, most states require early disclosure of alibis so prosecutors can check their validity.

FORGOT ANNIVERSARY

Tiffany's was closed.

———◆———

I left your present at the office.

———◆———

I celebrate the day we fell in love,
rather than the day we got married.

———◆———

I thought our anniversary was *next* August.

———◆———

It got stuck in customs, but it's on its way!

———◆———

I celebrate our marriage *every* day.

———◆———

I was too busy thinking about
your birthday present.

NOT MOVING IN

I don't want you to get too dependent on me.

———◆———

Your art will clash with mine.

———◆———

Your dog and I don't get along.

———◆———

My horoscope advises against it.

———◆———

I need a lot of "me" time.

FALLING ASLEEP IN AN
UNTIMELY MANNER

You just make me feel so safe and relaxed.

———◆———

I thought we were done.

The kids are just so exhausting.

———◆———

I'm still tired from the last time.

———◆———

It was the wine.

NOT IN THE MOOD

My hamstrings are too tight.

———◆———

I've got that "not so fresh" feeling.

———◆———

I talked to my mother tonight.

———◆———

I've got the *Sesame Street*
theme song stuck in my head.

I just got my euphemism.

I think I'm coming down with
something and I don't want you to catch it.

BREAKUPS

I'll just end up hurting you.

I don't want to ruin you for other people.

It's not you; it's the fact that
I can't stand being with you.

When you said you wanted to hear the "L-word,"
I thought you meant "leave."

I'm saving you the trouble of dumping me.

We just don't have the same taste in three-way partners: I like them, you don't.

My therapist says I need to be
on my own for a while.

It's because my parents didn't say they loved me.

YOU LOOK GREAT!

Go ahead. Say it. And know you're keeping the very fabric of society together. A study published in Proceedings of the Royal Society B found "prosocial," or white lies create closer ties within a social network versus "antisocial" lying for personal gain, which damages relationships. "The balance between prosocial and antisocial lies may set constraints on the structure of social networks, and hence the shape of society as a whole," researchers wrote.

We can never be together because
our names don't hyphenate well.

Look at it this way—now you get to keep the
half of the stuff you actually cared about anyway.

It's not you; it's your cat.

My shrink says your "me time"
involves way too much of my "me time."

CHILD TO PARENT

If I clean my room now, I'm just going
to have to clean it again in a few days.

I thought my phone was in my pocket,
but I left it in my locker.

It's not mine.

This is not a tantrum; it's a
reaction to your cruel failure to spoil me.

———◆———

I will eat my vegetables only when all
the children of the world get the broccoli
they deserve.

———◆———

My homework is to practice civil disobedience.

———◆———

If I don't sneak out of the house,
how will I learn about independence?

———◆———

We're just friends.

———◆———

Is that what that is? I've never even tried it.

It's just a different time now.

———————◆———————

Everybody's doing it.

———————◆—— ——

Nothing. Nowhere.

PARENT TO CHILD

Your dad and I were
just having a discussion.

———————◆———————

I did it once—but I regretted it immediately.

———————◆———————

Without my failings you kids wouldn't have
anything to blame your own on.

———————◆———————

Just be glad you didn't have my parents.

I was not a deadbeat dad—I was practicing
"non-invasive" parenting.

———————◆———————

You would have resented the hell out of me
if I was too much of a tiger mom.

———————◆———————

Don't worry; someday all this schoolyard teasing
will leave you with a chip on your shoulder that
will make you very rich.

———————◆———————

I wanted to help you improve your
problem-solving skills.

———————◆———————

Because we didn't know
any better back then.

———————◆———————

Because I said so, that's why.

AVOIDING CHORES

The vacuum cleaner was all the way upstairs.

———◆———

I've got a sensitivity to all
those cleaning products.

———◆———

I'm training the dog to take itself out.

———◆———

I wasn't sure you were ready
for me to clean that.

———◆———

I know you have your own special
way of putting my clothes away.

———◆———

I didn't wash the dishes
because we're conserving water.

Give it enough time and the garbage will just decompose into nothing sitting right where it is.

———◆———

Don't look at it as an "uncut lawn"—it's a "drought-tolerant native plant grassland preserve."

EXCUSING NON-ATTENDANCE

I couldn't stop binge-watching *Gilligan's Island*.

———◆———

I would've made it to the party, but my team was in the playoffs!

———◆———

My iCal got deleted during the iOS upgrade.

———◆———

No, I really love experimental mime theater, but my car broke down.

I just couldn't get the time off work to make it
to great-uncle Howard's retirement party.

I was drunk when you mentioned it
and I totally blacked out.

I forgot.

JUST SAY NO

Introverts are great at inventing excuses to
avoid social situations, but the experts say you
should actually simply say "No." Give it to them
straight—"I'm an introvert, I don't like large
groups, I don't like parties, I've been out too
many times this week, I'm happy at home with
Netflix and Fig Newtons." If they keep nudging
you to join them after you've been honest, then
you have every right to claim that you have a
communicable disease.

GETTING OUT OF INVITES

It's my bowling night.

I'm allergic to your cat.

Oh, the party is that Saturday?
I'm having my tires rotated.

I'm going to a top-secret corporate retreat
for the whole weekend.

Sorry, I don't do well in crowds.

I have to go to her family's
house for the holiday.

My dog doesn't look so good.

I'd love to see your daughter's holiday concert,
but I already made plans.

◆

My meds aren't strong enough.

◆

Your meds aren't strong enough.

EXPLAINING THE FAMILY

We're WASPs—we don't do family stuff.

◆

I come from a long line of non-huggers.
Don't take it personally.

◆

Just ignore Uncle Billy. He's from
a different generation.

◆

My mom's face just always looks like that.

Before we go in, I want you to know that I
disagree with everything my family stands for.

———————◆———————

It's not that my father doesn't like you;
he just doesn't like new people.

———————◆———————

My brother isn't dysfunctional.
He's just sensitive.

GENERAL BAD MANNERS

I'm sure she'll get over it in a few days.

———————◆———————

My house is too small to host.

———————◆———————

Since you're against materialism, I thought you'd
prefer not to get a Christmas gift this year.

You know me—I never send thank-you cards.

―――――◆―――――

I'm not avoiding your calls; I've just decided
to take a hiatus from technology.

―――――◆―――――

If I don't leave my phone on during
the movie, how will I post about it?

ROOMMATES

It looked just like the cleaning toothbrush.

―――――◆―――――

I was under the impression we shared
everything here, including boyfriends.

―――――◆―――――

I was so smashed I guess I
thought it was the bathroom.

"OFFICER, I CAN EXPLAIN..."

Children are known for lying, but we have to salute the ambition of one young Norwegian boy. Early one winter morning, this adventurous ten-year-old stole his parents' car, then with his baby sister in tow, started off towards his grandparents' house, about 38 miles away. When he drove off the road and ended up in a ditch, he claimed to be a dwarf who had forgotten his driver's license. This kid either has a future in theater—or in politics.

It's not my music that's too loud,
it's the walls that are too thin.

I ate what was in the fridge because
I wanted to help you on your diet.

Then why do they call it a "garbage disposal?"
The bags just clog it up.

AWKWARD MOMENTS

I thought you guys broke up!

———◆———

I just assumed you had been
invited to the party too.

———◆———

I told you that a long time ago!

———◆———

You're my best friend—and so is she.

POLITICAL CORRECTNESS

I was going to vote, but then I realized
that I don't live in a swing state and
I still have laundry to do.

———◆———

I volunteer every Thanksgiving.

I'll just have to wait to be more fuel efficient
until after the kids are grown and I don't
obviously need this minivan.

———————◆———————

I didn't forget the paper towels, I just think
we should start being mindful of our waste
and start using reusable towels.

———————◆———————

Biking to work? Where would I shower?

———————◆———————

I'd recycle if I knew what the numbers meant.

INGESTING SUBSTANCES

This pack doesn't count because
I bought it before I quit.

———————◆———————

Apparently cigarettes help
improve cognition.

I'll switch to menthols
first—they're disgusting.

This marijuana is medicinal.

I have a real doctor's prescription for this.

It's a sin to leave a bottle half-full.

That glass was a lot bigger
than I had originally thought.

I don't drink French amounts of wine.

Don't ask me how many I had…
you know I'm terrible at math.

In the old days, alcohol was considered medicine.

———◆———

I'm buying all this wine to entertain with.
For a very large dinner party.

———◆———

The antioxidants are good for you.

WEIGHT

I just haven't grown out of my baby fat.

———◆———

Weight Watchers has too much math.

———◆———

I'm just big boned.

———◆———

What you see here is just a setup for an
unbelievably dramatic "after" photo.

Vodka is carb-free.

I'd have to buy new clothes if I lost weight.

———◆———

Well, at least I'm not obese.

FOOD

If we weren't supposed to eat meat,
it wouldn't taste so darned good.

———◆———

I need meat to sustain
my substantial muscle mass.

———◆———

Potatoes are a plant, so, technically a vegetable.

———◆———

My dream diet's still out there somewhere.

The problem with good nutrition
is that it tastes nutritious.

———————◆———————

You'll see, soon science will tell us
to eat a lot more fat and carbs.

CAREER

Success is afraid of me.

———————◆———————

I don't want to overshadow my family.

———————◆———————

Getting a job would be giving in to The Man.

———————◆———————

For your information, it's called "multi-level
marketing," and I'm supposed to be getting my
first paycheck any day now.

NO ACCOUNTING
FOR TASTE

After repeatedly violating Idaho nudity laws, the owner of Boise's Erotic City strip club handed out sketchpads to patrons and called it "art night." The police saw things differently, citing three dancers for breaking the law—which only protects full nudity with "serious artistic merit." Said a police spokeswoman, "It was pretty obvious they were attempting to use artistic expression to get around the law." Sadly for the owner, the police didn't give extra credit for creativity.

Hey, I may not be fulfilled,
but at least it pays the bills.

◆

My grandmother came to me in a
dream to warn me away from law school.

In this economy, I'm just lucky
to have a full-time job.

———◆———

I'll ask for that raise the next time my boss is in
a good mood and Mercury isn't in retrograde.

———◆———

I'm going to start my book as
soon as the research is finished.

———◆———

I would've received that promotion,
but that other guy is such a suck-up.

LOVE

Once I get my finances squared away,
then I'll think about settling down.

———◆———

I'm too busy right now to date.

What? You think I should just settle?

———————◆———————

I just haven't met "Ms. Right."

———————◆———————

Why rush into a relationship?

IN TROUBLE ON THE ROAD

Oh, so that's the speedometer!

———————◆———————

I was showing my kids what
crappy driving looks like.

———————◆———————

I don't have a driver's license because
I am a citizen of the world.

———————◆———————

Why else do you think they call them bumpers?

My gas pedal was stuck—it's being
recalled by the manufacturer.

I guess at a certain point,
even non-alcoholic beer will get you drunk.

It depends on what your
definition of "stop" is, officer.

I leave the blinker on just in case
I have to change lanes.

I haven't had a thing to drink, officer.
Alcohol interferes with my medical marijuana.

That gas pedal looks an awful lot like the brake.

Officer, I was just asking for directions,
but she seemed really nice and we just hit it off.

———————◆———————

I passed you at that high rate of speed because
I'm on my way to the police station to donate to
the Policeman's Fund.

IN AN
INAPPROPRIATE PLACE

I'm doing research for my novel.

———————◆———————

I thought the sign said "sax" shop.

———————◆———————

I'm looking for a gag gift.

———————◆———————

I just come for the
conversation and camaraderie.

YOU'RE...SAFE!

Don't count on Larry David getting you sprung, but one very lucky guy hit that jackpot. Juan Catalan was in jail for five and a half months on murder charges before footage from David's HBO show *Curb Your Enthusiasm* helped free him. Turns out a scene that landed on the cutting-room floor showed Catalan at a Los Angeles Dodgers game at the time of the murder he allegedly committed. Almost sounds like a *Seinfeld* bit.

These dancers really just want to talk to
someone, and I can provide that.

The buffet is actually really good here.

IN SCHOOL

I was too busy trying to memorize
the world capitals. Ask me Burkina Faso!

Mind if I vape? Tests stress me out.

I thought this was an oral homework assignment.

I can't write anything
longer than 140 characters.

I didn't steal that. It's "found art."

My dog ate my router.

I don't trust spellcheck.

Plagiarism? I prefer to call my book report
the sincerest form of flattery.

I was texting the principal to tell her
what a brilliant rhetorician you are.

———————◆———————

My professor has it in for me.

———————◆———————

I had to delete everything in the cloud.

IN THE STORE

I figured you could always
use the practice folding clothes.

———————◆———————

That was a line? I thought you
were waiting for the restroom.

———————◆———————

I would've hung up all those things I tried on,
but I'm in such a hurry.

Sorry to hold everyone up, but I'm doing
my civic duty by putting all these pennies
back into circulation.

———————◆———————

The tomatoes at the bottom
of that stack looked so much fresher.

———————◆———————

Don't worry, I only have a few coupons.

BADLY BEHAVING PETS

I don't know what got into him.
He never does that.

———————◆———————

She just hates being on-leash.

———————◆———————

Oops—just used my last poop bag!

"The first thing I do in the morning is brush my teeth and sharpen my tongue."

—Oscar Levant